The Lindenwood Review

Issue 1 • 2011

LINDENWOOD UNIVERSITY

St. Charles, Missouri

Editor
Beth Mead

Managing Editor
Patricia Feeney

Assistant Editor
Charlene Engleking

Editorial Assistants
Nickolas Alexander, Cindy Allen, Carol Arnett, John Cunningham, Cynthia A. DuBois, Patricia Feeney, Anthony Clinton Green, Thomas Horan, Megan Ingram, DeAnna Jarrell Massie, Michelle Kehder, Tricia Sankey, Terry St. Clair

Logo Design • Cover Design • Journal Layout
Ad Design for Eve Jones, Catherine Rankovic, LU MFA, and TLR
Christopher Mead

Cover and Interior Photographs
Terry St. Clair

The Lindenwood Review is produced by the MFA in Writing Program at Lindenwood University and is published annually. Submissions are accepted from July 15 through December 15 each year. Email submissions to TheLindenwoodReview@lindenwood.edu. See full guidelines at http://TheLindenwoodReview.blogspot.com.

Subscriptions: Single issue: $7.00 • Two-year subscription (two issues): $12.00
To order, include your mailing address and make checks payable to Lindenwood University. Mail to:

The Lindenwood Review
Beth Mead, Editor
Lindenwood University
400 N. Kingshighway
St. Charles, Missouri 63301

ISBN   978-0-9846307-2-1
Copyright ©2011

http://LUmfa.webs.com
TheLindenwoodReview.blogspot.com

Issue 1 • 2011

LINDENWOOD UNIVERSITY
209 S. Kingshighway
St. Charles, Missouri 63301
www.lindenwood.edu

Contents

From the Editor

Ten minutes into my first class with the MFA students who helped produce this inaugural issue of *The Lindenwood Review,* the lights went out. We sat together in the dark, waiting for breakers to be flipped, and discussed the book we were about to create. Our eyes adjusted, and although we somehow felt an instant connection in the darkness of that windowless room, we eventually gathered up our books and went in search of an empty classroom, in search of light.

As the weeks went by and the snow piled up outside, we found ourselves still searching for that light, that flash of beauty or clarity or inventive language that caused a submitted piece to stand out from the rest. We were struck by the lush lyric prose of Irène Mathieu's "The Most Beautiful Woman I've Ever Seen," the strong narrative pull of "Naked" by Jenna Devine, and the concrete pain of "Tying Up the Replacement" by Ryan Stone. We were fascinated by Angie Chuang's glimpse into an Afghan home in her essay "On the Other Side of the Wall." We each championed pieces that affected us as readers, swept away by the manic energy of "The Saddest Tootsie Pop Ever" by Lisa Vaas and swallowed up by the lovely sadness of Christopher Linforth's "Moonbow." We read poetry submissions aloud in class, and each poem we selected for this issue stopped our breath, or made us laugh with joy, or even brought us to tears. Together, we created a book that we love.

This book would not have been possible without the help of many people. Sincere thanks to Lindenwood University President James Evans, Vice President Richard Boyle, and Vice President Jann Weitzel, whose input, approval, and support at the beginning of this process were invaluable. Thanks also to Spencer Hurst and Ana Schnellmann for their support of this new journal, to David Carkeet for his wisdom and guidance, and to Mary Troy and the staff of *Natural Bridge* for their assistance. We are also grateful to those who helped us toward the end of this process: Charlene Engleking for her editing skills and her thoughtful advice, Eve Jones and Julie Beard for their helpful contributions, and Chris Duggan, Public Relations Coordinator, for his tireless efforts on our behalf. Managing Editor Patricia Feeney's expertise, enthusiasm, and hard work are reflected in every page of this journal. Terry St. Clair provided the remarkable photographs of the Lindenwood University campus that appear on our cover and section headings, and Christopher Mead created a striking look for the journal with his design of our logo, cover, and interior layout.

My most heartfelt thanks go to the Issue 1 editorial assistants, the students in my class: Nickolas Alexander, Cindy Allen, Carol Arnett, John Cunningham, Cynthia A. DuBois, Patricia Feeney, Anthony Clinton Green, Thomas Horan, Megan Ingram, DeAnna Jarrell Massie, Michelle Kehder, Tricia Sankey, and Terry St. Clair. I am incredibly proud of these talented, insightful MFA students, and it was a pleasure to share this experience with them—reading until our eyes ached, fighting for work that we loved, and allowing ourselves to be moved by words, to let the pieces in this journal hit us hard, like a light in the dark.

Beth Mead

Fiction

Christopher Linforth

Moonbow

When I moved into apartment 4E, a grimy one-bed walkup on the Lower East Side, it wasn't for the view of the Coca-Cola billboard. It was more to do with my wife. She was jealous of my time in the office selling home insurance. I was lousy at it and rarely made more than two or three sales a day. Cold-calling retirement villages in Florida, I'd debate with the drunken supers the Gators' prospects and the fallibility of the BCS ratings. For hours we'd compare stats: receiving yards, sacks, interceptions, passing, rushing. In the evenings, I'd make small-talk with Omaha housewives. We'd chat about the tan leather sofas at Nebraska Furniture Mart and the new summer collection at Von Maur. After work I'd take the subway back to the renovated brownstone I shared with my wife in Astoria, a couple of blocks from the East River. A year back we'd remodeled the building after watching home improvements shows on TLC. I took out loans to rewire the electrics, re-sand the hardwood floors, and import a dining room set from Italy.

By the time the improvements were finished we'd developed a strange arrangement of sharing the space. The bedroom and bathroom were hers. I only had a temporary pass to brush my teeth and floss. However, the small study at the back of the house was mine. It had a view of the communal garden, shared by the neighborhood residents. From my position I could see the small pond dotted with lilies, the porch swing half-hidden in the shade of a ginkgo tree, and the beds of daises and roses overcome with wild hydrangea. At night, as the street light came through the study window, I sorted through my father's old collection of art prints and tried to put them in an order he would have approved. For years, he'd assembled a portfolio of European work, including a fine Picasso lithograph. Often, after arranging the prints in a chronological or alphabetical manner, or in terms of market value, I fell asleep in my beat-up recliner and started the cataloging again the next day.

When I saw my wife, our once sweet talk was reduced to an awkward system of qualifiers: "maybe," "perhaps," and often, "I have to check my work schedule." She berated me for not keeping our tentative dinner plans, or attending the theater with her friends, or visits to see her parents. She came from a wealthy family who lived in Rochester. Her mother and father drove matching his-and-hers Mercedes C-Class sedans to the country club to play tennis with seasoned pros. In the past I had often seen them enjoy post-game cocktails in the lounge, their talk centering on a lake house purchase in the Ozarks.

One evening my wife changed the brownstone's locks. For an hour I stood on the steps and tried to reason with her. She would only communicate through the intercom: "Why don't you have a better job?" she screamed. For her, this was the crux of our relationship. She was embarrassed by my lowly job title, and incensed by my refusal to apply for a promotion. The issue followed us into the bedroom: the last time we'd had sex was months before when she wanted kids and I said I would think about it.

In a coffee shop, near the brownstone, I studied the classifieds. One ad described a rent-controlled walk-up near the J line. I met the landlord in the tenement's lobby. He was a short man who liked to have an unlit cigar in his mouth and spoke in short pulses. "Sure thing," he repeated several times as we agreed on the lease. He looked anxious as he directed me away from checking out the neighborhood and particularly the abandoned garment warehouse opposite. I liked the old redbrick building and the large billboard on the flanking wall that faced the apartment. The advertisement seemed to have been replaced countless times as its rips and holes revealed the same faded image underneath: a 1950s-style picture of a full Coca-Cola glass with the word *Zing!* emerging from the bubbles.

For the first couple of weeks I slept on a cot borrowed from my brother and bought microwavable hamburgers and burritos from the deli at the corner. After work I'd get some whiskey from the liquor store and collapse into my battered recliner for an hour or two, the air conditioning on full to dry my sweat and block the sound of traffic outside. When the TV worked the weatherman talked about the late summer heat wave and the dust particulate coming in from the west. When it didn't work I took walks through the neighborhood to Hamilton Fish Park and thought about how I was going to get out of my situation. I would circle the large swimming pool, taking several minutes to complete one loop. Often I felt sorrier for myself than the destitute kids who swam in their underwear and the homeless men who slept on the benches.

Although the park didn't have the same ramshackle beauty as the garden, it came to be a place I'd go on the weekends. I'd sit on the grass near the entrance and watch couples and families come in and spread out rugs or towels on the ground for picnics and sunbathing. There was something idyllic about the sunlight glancing off their tan bodies and the secret bottles of wine shared in bright red Dixie cups. The intimate conversations and playful touches to the arm and knee left me sick. Often I had to look away and go back to my apartment for a whiskey.

It was after one of these trips to the park when I first heard my neighbor. His words were barely discernible, just a faint echo through the cheap brickwork that separated our apartments. He had a strange tone, broad but choppy, like his voice box was generating noise through a blender. For a while I tried to listen at the wall, but he always directed his monologues away from my position. I learned that if I opened my window and sat on the inner ledge, I could make out his words. There were often rants about the city's tax system. He especially liked to repeat "They're always screwing us working stiffs" as though he was one. Sometimes he was eloquent and learned, giving recitations of Shakespearean soliloquies. The strange emphases he put on Hamlet's "To die, to sleep" and "To grunt and sweat under a weary life" were unnatural, often leading me to turn up the TV. However, it was his quieter moments, his murmuring about meteorological phenomena, which caught my interest. At length he would read out long tables of atmospheric pressure, and then link the high altitude results to something I'd never heard of: moonbows.

The word intrigued me, and when my wife shipped my possessions across town, it was my childhood encyclopedia that I first dug out from under my cut-up suits. The short entry read: *Moonbow: A lunar rainbow. See Rainbow (lunar)*. Unfortunately the R section was damaged, torn and stained a dark pink from a two-decade ago Kool-Aid accident. Still my imagination filled in the gaps, a speculation that it was a rainbow formed by the moon's, and not the sun's, light.

My neighbor came back to this topic regularly, around two or three times a week. "Purity," he said one day. "A line to God," he said on another. The evening he mentioned God, I was sitting between packing crates filled with my father's art print collection. As he continued his lengthy description of the perfect moonbow, I took notes about the brightness of the moon, my position relative to the moon (I needed it behind me), the optimal rain conditions, and the darkness of the sky. According to my understanding the darkness was, of course, the biggest problem. The lights in the city were far too bright to see this phenomenon. Even if I turned off the apartment lights and decreased the glow of the city by a magnitude of ten, there would be still no chance I could see one. For days I thought about a solution. Somehow I'd have to have a complete absence of all artificial light. Any practical way of achieving this was beyond my high school education, and for a while I gave up on ever seeing a moonbow.

A few days after this low point the divorce proceedings began and I took up smoking in the evenings. I'd perch on the window ledge, half in, half out. I wasn't afraid of the drop as the ground below seemed to offer at least one answer. I didn't want to die, but I was bored with my new life. My neighbor's speeches offered some respite, and I came to depend on them for intellectual stimulation. Once, when I leaned quite far out, I caught a glimpse of him. He was a pale man, older than me, his hair graying at the temples and balding on top. I edged back into the apartment. I wasn't sure whether he had seen me. He'd been sitting on some sort of chair next to his window, his face vacant. I smoked two more cigarettes before I dared look out again. He was still there; this time he did see me. He looked alarmed, perhaps even frightened, and he rolled backward in what I could now see was a wheelchair.

I felt guilty, but not so guilty that I immediately went around apologizing. I thought if I waited a day or two it would give me an air of nonchalance, an indication to him that I hadn't been spying, that it had all been a great misunderstanding. As the weeks passed the impulse to visit him left me. I enjoyed listening to him too much. He was like a disembodied spirit trapped in some other world. I even moved my bed closer to the wall so I could lie in it and close my eyes, his voice drifting into my head.

One Sunday afternoon, sometime later, I saw him again as I walked home from the park. At his open window he was studying the Coca-Cola billboard and the two workmen replacing the neon tubes that framed the advertisement. He wore a black sweater vest, a military green button-down shirt underneath. He had a stiff posture as he leaned forward, his hands gripping the bottom of the window frame. I thought I saw desperation or possibly boredom. From my limited angle, it was difficult to tell what was going through his mind. I attempted a half-wave, but backed out and ran my hand through my hair. He saw me and moved backwards into his apartment.

In the evening I had a couple of drinks as I argued with my wife on the phone. She wanted me to sign over the brownstone to her in exchange for the Picasso. I told her I was busy and that she should talk to my lawyer. After she hung up, I grabbed a couple of beers from my fridge and stepped into the hallway to speak to the neighbor. With the first knock my weeks-earlier plan of nonchalance went to hell. I knocked too lightly and so on the second attempt I overcompensated, banging hard on the door like some madman locked away in a Victorian sanatorium. After a few seconds I heard the metallic squeak of his wheels as he rolled closer.

"Who is it?" he said.

I leaned close to the door, swearing that I could hear his breathing on the other side. "It's your neighbor."

"What do you want?"

This question stumped me. What did I want? What was I doing here? Why didn't I stay in my apartment and drink another whiskey and Coke? I thought about backing away, returning to my recliner and *Sunday Night Football*. I almost convinced myself that he wouldn't notice, that he would put it down to kids, weak-willed social services, or immigrants. "It's your neighbor, Robert. Robert Black," I found myself saying.

"And?"

"I want to apologize for before. You know, me seeing you at the window and not waving."

The door opened slightly to reveal his sallow gray face and a pair of bifocals mounted on top of his head. I bent down and offered him a beer through the two-inch gap.

He brought down his glasses to study the bottle of Bud Light. "I don't touch the stuff," he said. "So, who are you?"

"As I said, I'm your neighbor. I've been meaning to come around the last couple of weeks. But you know, with work and all."

He snorted and then coughed up some phlegm. He spit it into a pocket handkerchief, probably monogrammed with his initials. After a short pause he unhooked the chain, and I entered with the smile I used to give my wife, a kind of upended grimace.

His apartment had two bedrooms (both bigger than mine) and a clean kitchen that opened up into a large living room, organized so he could easily move around it. Against the wall stacks of shoe boxes were labeled in a regimented manner: newspapers (1980-85), newspapers (1986-1990), letters (Martha), letters (Mother), state maps (no Alaska or Hawaii), state maps (Alaska and Hawaii), certificates (achievements), certificates (government and state), weather reports (national), weather reports (local). Yet for all the room's efficiency the decor was unfashionable, a kind of orange rust wallpaper patterned with elongated roses, and in the center of the room a Formica coffee table slightly chipped at the edges. On top of it were well-thumbed weather-related periodicals that had titles like *The Meteorological Magazine* and *Storms Monthly*.

He rolled to the window, his wheelchair stopping over two grooves in the floor, where, I could tell, he sat day after day. Nearby on the nightstand were camouflage-patterned binoculars, a thick black flashlight, an open pack of batteries, and a cup of coffee that looked weeks old.

I drew up a stool so we were the same height. "As I said earlier, I'm sorry. I like to smoke on the ledge and—"

"Do you have a spare?"

"Yeah, sure." I passed him one along with my lighter.

"It's been years since I had one of these." He lit the cigarette, bent forward, arm resting on the ledge, and smoked. He coughed a little as he took deep drags, holding the smoke in a few seconds longer than I'd ever done. Afterward, he carried on talking as though his small indulgence had never happened. "So, what do you do?"

"I sell insurance."

"Sounds like a waste."

"It has its moments."

He made a strange noise, a sort of lengthened huff. "Army man myself," he said afterwards. "Cartographer with the Corp. of Engineers."

"Interesting work?"

"We created military maps. I used reconnaissance photographs, local intel, and available data to draw enemy installations, roads, and airfields, onto a master copy. At the Pusan Perimeter, that's in Korea by the way, my work was commended by General Walker. It got me promoted twice by the end of my service."

I noticed he wouldn't look at me when he spoke, only at the view outside, which was the same as mine. I conjectured that he could see a small degree more of the park. I was a little jealous of the section of dry grass, the late sun on the pool, and the old women with poofed-up hair walking their Mal-Shi and Bichon Frise, oblivious to anyone else.

"How long have you lived here?" I asked.

"Since I retired," he said, picking up his binoculars. He looked through them, out to some spot in the distance. "Perhaps too long," he added after a while.

"I know what you mean. I'm not sure I fit into this neighborhood."

"Think you're too good?"

"It's not that." I finished the second of my beers and stood up to leave. He waved me down and I noticed the thinness of his arms, muscled and veiny.

"My wife died a couple of years ago," he said, resting the binoculars in his lap. "We had been living in this neighborhood for fifteen or so years, something like that. She was the one who kept track of these things."

I wanted to tell him that he was lucky, that women—despite their benefits—were no good. Instead, I nodded and asked him what had happened.

"A car accident on FDR. A Hummer clipped our car and she drove into the barrier. She got a steel pole in her head. I was left with this." He gestured to his legs, which I could see were thin and useless.

I thought about telling him I was sorry, that I was a jerk for asking, and that it would be good if I left. But I said nothing and listened to the rest of the story: He survived on his veteran benefits and an income from the insurance settlement. That money bought him a helper, who delivered meals three times a day, helped him wash, dress, and use the bathroom, and wheeled him one Sunday a month to the Catholic church a block away. He didn't strike me as particularly religious. He displayed only one cross in the apartment, above his boxes, probably nailed there by someone else. But there was something about his conviction in the things he talked about, an evangelical passion for the life he used to lead that intrigued me the most.

Our relationship developed over the next couple of months. I would stop by once or twice a day to check on him, bring him a pack of Camels, and listen to his long lectures. He would talk for what seemed like hours at a time. I asked questions, but in truth he barely noticed me. Almost by accident I found out his name was John. One day, while retrieving my mail from the lobby, I looked over to his apartment number. I saw the mailbox originally read Mr. and Mrs. John Wallinger, but someone had used a Sharpie to scrawl over the neat handwriting, leaving a big J.W.

Apart from the first conversation about his wife, he rarely spoke about anything personal. A couple of times I mentioned my wife, her paranoia, or at least her way of legally receiving a quick divorce. She was claiming adultery, naming one of my co-workers, who was older than my mother and had a penchant for sudoku and chamomile tea, as my lover. John would refuse to process these talks. Rather, he would focus the attention on the weather patterns he could see outside: electrical storms, blizzards, and most often, rain clouds. He created his own classification based upon visibility and the amount of water that would pool on the sidewalk. His terms ranged from "a panhandler's spit" to "Biblical flood." He kept the results in a notebook, often drawing elaborate graphs and circling the days and times of unstable weather.

In a moment of openness, one late Monday evening, he recalled he loved night rain the most, as it was the greatest chance to see a moonbow.

"Have you ever seen one?" I asked him.

"Nope," he replied. "The conditions here are against it. You would have to go somewhere like Hawaii, or New Zealand, or even one of the National Parks out west. I've seen pictures. They're beautiful, usually a white curve, low in the sky." He rotated his upper body to his boxes and opened one labeled Moon (Light). He spent a few minutes sorting through a pile of official-looking documents, newspaper clippings, and some typed-up notes. "Here we go," he said, passing over a small photograph.

I examined the image. It was a black and white landscape that had dark gray mountains and the outline of a pine forest. High above was an arc of brilliant white.

"We should plan a trip," I said.

He moved over to the window and pulled down the blinds with a hard tug. "I can't leave here."

"We can work past your disability."

"My disability has nothing to do with it." His eyes locked on to the photograph of him and his wife that hung on the bedroom door. "Martha didn't like the outdoors. She hated bugs. Anything that bit her gave her a rash."

My wife had dropped the adultery allegations and hired a private detective to search through my affairs for something else she could use. "At least she wasn't a parasite, like mine," I said. John seemed irked but I carried on talking hoping to recover the situation. "If we leave the city, you'll get a chance to see a moonbow. Maybe she would have wanted that."

"You don't know anything."

"When's the last time you went outside?"

He snatched the moonbow picture from my hand. "Get out," he said.

I didn't push the issue for a few days. I wanted John to go with my plan. We both had nothing to lose, and I hadn't been on a trip since my fifth wedding anniversary a couple of years back. Yet however much I put it to him that we could leave the city and head out west to see one, he refused, citing everything from the bad traffic to the late arrival of his morning newspaper. I could tell he didn't want to talk about the real reason, about the death of his wife. At night, when I was in bed, sometimes I could hear him shuffling through papers and moving to his window, the familiar sound of a lighter clicking and him smoking. I imagined, as he looked out, that he would think about his wife, about the life he used to have.

As Thanksgiving approached I met John's helper in the hallway. She was older than John, perhaps an impression caused by her thinning hair and pastel beige cardigan. She clutched to her chest a torn pocketbook, stuffed with coupons for Pedigree Good Bites. She introduced herself as June.

"Are you the new neighbor?" she asked.

"That's right."

She looked down at my bare feet and seemed baffled by my lack of socks and shoes. "I'm worried about his health," she said. "He has mood swings and he coughs all the time. It might be the onset of TB."

Almost laughing as I held a carton of cigarettes for John, I said, "I'll talk to him about it."

She gave me a disapproving look and took to the stairs.

I let myself into John's with the spare key he'd given me for the cigarette runs. Inside, he was reorganizing his stack of boxes by writing new labels for a new top layer focused on natural disasters. He'd already marked out Earthquakes (Northern Hemisphere), Earthquakes (Southern Hemisphere), Tidal Waves (Asian), and Nuclear Fallout (Military), and had six more that were blank. As he wrote on the next label his hand spasmed and his Sharpie fell to the floor.

"June might be onto your smoking," I said, picking the pen up and handing it to him.

"She worries about me," he said, sticking the Global Warming (Hoax) label on the box in front. "Some days she reminds me of Martha." From the folder on his lap he took out some newspaper clippings and put them into the box. "I found some data on sea level decreases. But you'll never read about it in *The New York Times*."

"I'm pretty sure the icecaps are melting."

"It's a con, a liberal attempt to raise taxes on the sly for welfare." He rolled to the window and picked up his binoculars. He pointed them at the park, and as I followed him over, we both saw a drab yellow school bus pull up near the park entrance. A group of Down syndrome kids and their parents slowly exited the bus and then walked into the park.

"We should go, too."

"That's not a good idea."

"We can use the maintenance elevator at the end of the hall."

"What am I? A trash can?"

I held up the carton of Camels. "You can have these if you come with me." I saw the weakness in his face: he rubbed his temples and pushed back the gray tufts above his ears. "We'll be back in an hour and then you can sit here and rant all you want."

I pushed his wheelchair to the park. He'd resisted at first, but after fifty yards he tired himself out and said he was taking a nap. He was lighter than I thought, barely ninety pounds, and it took only a few minutes to reach the entrance. He remained silent. But as we passed through the gates he raised his hand for us to stop, then he lowered it, as he saw the grass lawns and line of trees that led to the pool. Perhaps, like me, he could smell the strange mix of pollen and chlorine, a smell that brought back childhood and after-school trips with my father.

We circled the pool slowly, his wheelchair gliding over the smooth concrete edge. The water seemed translucent, a kind of odd blue that captured the sunlight and kept it trapped at the pool's bottom. Gentle waves lapped against the curb. Orange leaves, small knobby twigs, and dead wasps and flies rode the crests. In the shallow end, the kids from the bus were in bright orange life jackets splashing and laughing.

"My wife is dating someone," I said as we completed one loop.

"Women died in Pusan. Civilian casualties, they called them."

I wasn't sure if he was trying to cheer me up or if he was just remembering the war. "Did you see this happen?"

"My maps got them incinerated."

I stopped pushing and took out my flask and gave it to him. Without thanking me he took two long swigs and kept the flask clasped in his lap.

I wanted to say something deep or intelligent or even just leave him there with his thoughts. For whatever reason I had nothing, and I sat down on the concrete and together we watched the sun set over the water.

After work the next day I enjoyed a few drinks with my colleagues and I told them about John. I described moonbows, but most assumed I had invented them. Almost as a joke, my boss suggested that I should secretly organize a trip and then strong-arm John into it. I said I would. Later that evening, on the way home, I stopped at Port Authority to buy two Greyhound tickets to Yosemite. With boyhood glee I kept fingering the tickets in my pocket and thought about the possibilities that awaited us. I imagined a deserted spot in the park, near one of the waterfalls or hot pools. We'd be far away from John's memories and my wife. At night we'd sit and wait for the rain and wait for the arc to form. The city would be behind us.

Through the streets to my building, an icy wind carried the smell of pretzels and the sound of far-off sirens. Back at my tenement I was still half-delirious and took the stairs two at a time. When I reached my floor I sensed something was wrong. I saw John's front door was open, and a cop was inside his apartment looking out of the window. He turned when he heard me, but I brushed past him to see for myself. John's body was flat and lifeless on the sidewalk, his face half-submerged in a puddle. I wish I could say there was a reflection, an arc of white light from the C of the Coca-Cola billboard. But there wasn't, just bubbles of spit and blood in the dark oily water.

He left no note. The newspapers hypothesized it was suicide, a long-standing guilt for his wife's death compounded by the holiday season. Later the coroner could not dismiss this, but ruled it an accident, a mishap when John leaned too far out of the window, probably to smoke a cigarette.

The day after the funeral the landlord agreed I could switch leases. He just said, "Sure," and chewed on his cigar. It took a while to move all my stuff into the apartment. I felt guilty about erasing John's presence. Eventually, though, the transition was complete and I got the Picasso on the wall, right where the cross used to be. The strange lines and rectangular demarcations of the lithograph were an odd reminder of my old life. Sometimes, when I look at the picture and then at the park outside the window, I can never be sure which version of his death was the truth. I like to think he had seen what he was after, and had tried to get it.

Naked

Dahlia felt a certain dizziness, the rush of a twenty-five-year-old memory, as she let herself be jostled through the crowd in the museum's vast atrium. Overhead the sun was setting and streaks of orange burned through the glass ceiling, painting strips of light on top of the heads moving into the main gallery. The glow combined with her nerves cast a strange aura about the room. The colors were too saturated, the blues and greens too bright.

"Dahlia."

Harry's hand slipped into hers and anchored her momentarily. "I keep losing you in this crowd."

She tightened her grip on his hand. "Sorry. It's packed. I had no idea it would be so popular."

Harry chuckled. "The opening of E.M. Gregory's new show? I'm surprised they don't have riot police guarding the place."

Dahlia smiled faintly at him. She knew it was only a matter of time before he slipped into his art history professor voice and started marveling at the brushstrokes or chiaroscuro techniques in a still life. She knew this, and she loved him for it. But she had not come to see E.M. Gregory's new show, to marvel at the never-before-seen works exhibited for the first time in a posthumous tribute to the artist. She had only come to see one painting in particular, one in E.M. Gregory's series of nudes that *The New York Times* had dubbed "an exquisite and breathtaking view into the human psyche."

Harry was already walking forward, tugging her along like an eager child. He had taught a seminar on Gregory and his contemporaries, and Dahlia could tell that the chance to see these previously unknown works made him almost giddy with excitement. She wished she could match his enthusiasm, but a sharp twist of fear behind her ribs inhibited her. The entrance to the gallery loomed ahead, a massive black-and-white photograph of the artist suspended above the glass double doors. Dahlia could feel the enormous eyes on her as she followed Harry through the crowd. E.M. Gregory was young in this picture, maybe thirty. Definitely taken before the decade of heavy drinking that would put ghosts in his eyes and carve gorges in his olive skin. It was a photograph from the time she knew E.M. Gregory—before he was E.M. Gregory, when he was still Elliot and she was his model.

Maybe there were a million reasons why she did it. She was young, she was impetuous. It was the summer before her senior year of college, her last chance at carefree living before graduation and impending adulthood. She had only just moved out of her parents' home into a real apartment—no more dorm rooms for her—and had paid her own rent for the first time that morning. Seeing her name shine in the wet black ink on the check gave her a restless tingle in the backs of her knees. Her legs propelled her from her apartment, down four flights of stairs, onto the sidewalk and into the sultry air. It was New York City in August; she could taste the melting asphalt with every intake of breath. The midday sun glared off the skyscrapers and left her coated in a sheen of sweat that clung to the back of her neck and the hollow in her collarbone like a second skin. So maybe this was the only reason she did it: the heat.

The ad was tacked to the bulletin board outside the university student center, its bottom fringed into little tear-off scraps with a name and a number. She had been hoping to find a free movie screening or a jazz concert, but instead she found the ad. NUDE MODEL NEEDED FOR PAINTER, it read. Pays $8/hour.

Dahlia worked part time as a waitress. She could use the money. And it was so damn hot.

Her parents were salt-of-the-earth, no-nonsense Lutherans. Her mother taught Sunday school; her father sang in the church choir. They would die if they knew their daughter was taking off her clothes for money. But Dahlia was a grown woman. She was slender and pretty; why shouldn't someone paint her? She tore off the slip of paper and dug into her purse for change. Maybe if the ad hadn't been posted next to a pay phone, she would have shoved the number in her back pocket and forgotten about it. But the opportunity beckoned to her, so she dropped a quarter in the slot and dialed. She would wonder later how she'd missed it, that tremor, the balance of her universe shifting ever so slightly.

"God, Dahlia, this is amazing," Harry said, halting suddenly in front of a portrait of a little boy. Dahlia felt dizzy. A quick glance around the room confirmed that this was a safe place. Landscapes and clothed figures. She exhaled. The nudes hung in a room beyond here.

"Look at the eyes. I've never seen anything like it." He edged closer to the painting and leaned forward, his hands clasped behind his back. Dahlia steadied herself on his shoulder.

"Explain it to me," she said. This was her line. She had been saying it since she met Harry twenty-four years ago, when he was still a graduate student in art history at Columbia. He was the TA for her Early Christian Art class; she came to his office for help on an essay and left with dinner plans. She was hesitant about their relationship at first, until he revealed that he had flunked art in high school. He possessed no artistic talent whatsoever, but he worshipped Botticelli the way some people worship God. He took her to art museums on weekends and gestured rapturously at his favorite paintings, explaining the significance of each flower or perfectly arranged apple. Dahlia let him lead her through these exhibits, marveling at how Harry could find something new to say about each of the myriad crucified Christs and their respective bloodied extremities.

"The eyes are almost glimmering," Harry said, gesturing to the boy's face. "You just know in the next second he was going to stick his tongue out or throw a water balloon at you. This isn't just a frozen moment, it's vital and alive."

He started to go on about the juxtaposition of something with the temporal immediacy of something else, but Dahlia had already tuned out. She was already imagining the life story of this little boy. The painting was titled *John, 5, Sitting*. She wondered where John was now, if his hair was still cornsilk yellow or if it had darkened with age. He would be about thirty now. Maybe his mother kept a copy of the portrait in the living room. Maybe he was here in this museum right now. Or maybe he never knew that Elliot had become E.M. Gregory and had no idea that thousands of people were awestruck by this single image of him as a child.

Dahlia had not possessed any desire for such fame or immortality. She was expecting nothing more than a good story to tell at a bar to her girlfriends or future suitors. In fact, she had assumed that this guy would be a typical New York starving *artiste*, the kind who did bad Cubist portraits of meth dealers with paint made of his own blood and complained that nobody understood his aesthetic.

But his voice on the phone was soft and free of pretension. He gave her the address of his studio and told her to come by on the weekend. She walked the ten blocks that Saturday, still not fully aware of what she had gotten herself into, and buzzed 62B. It was only when she stood at the threshold of his apartment that she realized she was going to be naked in a strange man's home. Heat flooded her face. By the time he got the door open she was trying not to hyperventilate.

He was very handsome. Even in her terror she couldn't help but see that. His eyes were sea-glass green and he had two-day stubble on his face.

"You must be Dahlia," he said. "I'm Elliot."

Her hand was sweating, but she could not avoid the handshake. Her fingers left damp slug trails on his palm. He stepped out of the way so she could come into the apartment. It was a strangely intimate moment; she felt like his lover or his mistress. Had she shaved her legs that morning? She wondered if her underwear waistband would leave a mark on her skin.

Elliot was talking, explaining something about this project and his summer classes at Pratt. She followed him numbly into what she assumed must be his studio. It smelled faintly chemical. There were canvases propped up along the walls, palettes balanced on every flat surface, industrial lights clamped to metal stands. She noticed a twin-sized mattress shoved into the corner, its dark blue sheets crumpled. There was also a narrow kitchen, divided from the rest of the room by a waist-high countertop. Mundane realities like sleep and sustenance were pushed to the outskirts of the room; it was clear his real love was here, centered amid the turpentine and tubes of paint.

He dragged a forest green couch to the middle of the room. Late afternoon sunlight poured in from the skylight overhead.

"So, if you don't mind, I'd like to get started soon, before I lose the light."

A few moments passed before Dahlia realized she was supposed to respond to this.

"Oh, yeah. Sure."

"Would you like anything to drink? Water, tea?"

Dahlia would have preferred whiskey, but she just shook her head.

"All right, then," he said. "I'll step out for a moment and let you get ready."

She could not tell what would be worse: Elliot leaving now and re-entering when she was naked, or him witnessing the undressing. The door clicked closed behind him with an air of finality. Okay. Clothes, off. She considered this. Leave them at the foot of the couch, for easy access? Or fold them neatly and leave them on the table? There was a bathrobe draped over an empty easel—was she supposed to put that on? And what, take it off again when he came back in?

Suddenly she realized she had been standing frozen for a solid thirty seconds. What if he came back in when she was only halfway undressed? Her faced heated up again. In a panic she stepped out of her underwear and kicked them aside. Now the dress, which zipped up the back. The logistics of stripping had not occurred to her that morning. She almost dislocated her elbow trying to tug the damn thing down. It fell in a crumpled heap around her ankles. Lastly, the bra. She unhooked the clasp in one motion and tucked it under the dress. There. Naked.

The room seemed too big. She was usually only naked in her four by six bathroom, the walls close enough to contain her, to keep her safe. She wrapped her thin arms around her chest and perched on the edge of the couch, remembering childhood bathtimes, folding in on herself for warmth while her mother tested the heat of the water.

Now what? Was she supposed to pose herself, to arrange herself becomingly on the couch? Was he going to come back on his own, or was she supposed to call him back? She waited a few more seconds, listening for creaks in the floor that would indicate his approach. It was hard to hear over her blood pounding in her ears. She decided against the posing and remained as she was, prim and terrified, knees clamped together.

"Um," she said finally. "I'm ready."

Gooseflesh prickled on her legs as cool air rushed into the room. Elliot strode in and went right to his paints, barely noticing the naked woman on his couch. She couldn't tell whether to be insulted or relieved. She watched his back as he sifted through tubes of paint.

"Can you believe how hot it is?" he said. "I mean, even for August."

"Yeah," she croaked. Was she really talking about the weather with a man who could see her nipples?

He turned back to her with a fistful of brushes in one hand and a palette balanced on the other. She tried to remember how to unlock her joints.

"All right," he said, his face popping into view again. "If you could lie down on the couch."

It took a moment for her limbs to obey. She lifted her feet off the floor as if they were joined at the ankles and set them on the couch. She had to uncross her arms for balance and her breasts escaped.

"Stretch out a bit more? Right hand resting on your forehead, left on your collarbone."

It was like playing Twister in Russian. She couldn't figure out her directions for a full second.

"Great, just like that. Now relax."

She almost choked out a terrified giggle. Relax. Right. Her heart thumped a deliberate rhythm. *Why. Why. Why. Why.*

"All right," he said again. "Eyes on me. Good. Now hold still."

That part she could do. Her whole body was tensed into this position of repose. It occurred to her that this was the first man to see her wholly naked. Of course there had been the high school boys and their awkward, fumbling hands trying to work out the mechanics of her bra, the bold ones who even made it so far as the zipper of her jeans, but not one of them had ever gotten this far. Then again, she had taken off her clothes herself. She didn't know if this was something to be proud of or just pathetic.

Maybe a half hour later, the muscles in her neck relaxed. There was only so long one could be terrified. The fact of her nakedness slipped briefly out of her consciousness when she realized she was watching him as much as he was watching her. He had told her to keep her eyes on him, so she had an excuse to stare while he worked. She followed his gaze as it moved over the contours of her body. It was neither the lustful eye of a lover nor the clinical one of a doctor. He was very professional. He lingered just long enough to dab the paint onto the canvas before moving on.

She thought about this curious relationship, the mutual gazing. Dahlia had been taught not to stare, to keep her eyes on the straight and narrow. But here she had license to watch and to see! She studied Elliot as he worked. He was left-handed. Dried paint crusted the edges of his fingernails. He dabbed his brush on his bare arm as he went along, until there was a whole rainbow of smudges arcing over his wrist. She became very attuned to what he was doing; she could tell by the rhythm of his hand when he was blocking out a broad expanse of canvas and when he was detailing the shadows of her face.

The light was almost gone now. She guessed maybe two hours had passed. Elliot set his palette down.

"I think that's all for today," he said. "I'll let you get dressed."

He left the room and she put her feet on the floor. Well. She had done it. Surprisingly, she didn't ache with stiffness. Somewhere along the way she had relaxed, and standing up now felt a little like getting up from a nap. A giggle escaped her mouth and percolated in the silence. For a moment she gave in to the giddiness and shook out her whole body, reveling in the ridiculousness of the situation. She was naked! It seemed depressing to think about putting her dress back on. She had tasted courage and freedom and walking out of this apartment dressed properly seemed schoolmarmish and staid. With some reluctance, she stepped back into her underwear and pulled the dress on over her head, noticing the texture of the cotton on her skin. It felt strange.

There was a knock on the door.

"Come in," she said, wondering briefly if there would be some kind of morning-after awkwardness between them.

But of course there wasn't, because Elliot was a professional. He came into the room with an envelope of cash. He thanked her and told her she'd been a great model and that he'd be in touch about scheduling further sessions. Dahlia left a little lightheaded. There was something so mercenary about their goodbye. He had seen her naked and made art from her image. She had ventured into new territory, tested her limits. But the money cheapened this feeling somehow, reducing the entire experience to a simple transaction. She felt less like a muse than a whore.

It was only when she was back in her own apartment, taking off her clothes in the dim light of her bathroom, that she realized she had not even seen the painting.

Harry's excitement had reached new levels.

"It's incredible," he said, gesturing around the room. "This is just his student work, and already you can see him growing out of the derivative, art-school stuff. His own style is emerging—the characteristic brush stroke, the ecstatic use of color—amazing. Just amazing."

Dahlia felt him bouncing slightly on the balls of his feet. The action was incongruous with his thick-rimmed glasses and sweater vest. For a moment he seemed to her a child in a grown man's clothing. His eyes were a little wild as he surveyed the rest of the paintings, trying to decide where to go next. He was distressed, and Dahlia knew it was because he wanted to spend the rest of the evening in front of *John, 5, Sitting*, and also wanted to see every single work in the exhibition. She felt a sudden surge of affection for him. It was distant, as if he were a character in a movie who had done something charming. Harry did not know this, of course, but she felt this way about him often. Sometimes when they were at dinner parties, separated by a room full of people, she would mouth to herself, "That's my husband." Husband. As if saying it out loud would finally make it real to her. She watched her hand now as he pulled her to the next portrait. It didn't seem to belong to her.

Dahlia had wanted Elliot to call again, only because she wanted to see his progress on the first painting. She owed it to herself. One more session, then she would be done for good.

And maybe if Dahlia had been a terrible model, if her knees had never loosened up, if she carried more tension in her mouth, Elliot would not have called again. But as it turned out, she was a good model, and Elliot asked her to pose the next weekend. And the weekend after that, and the one after that.

Dahlia never quite got over the terror that thrilled through her when Elliot left her alone to get undressed, but it became a strange sort of high for her. She loved the feeling of the adrenaline seeping away, the heaviness settling into her limbs. Three or four hours of posing became meditative. Elliot stopped giving her cash.

"Just write up a tab," she told him. Once the uncomfortable monetary situation was out of sight, she began to enjoy herself.

As it turned out, she never told her girlfriends this story, even when they went out together for their weekly Friday happy hour. It just didn't seem like something you told a bunch of tipsy girls clutching margaritas. And even if she had wanted to tell them, she didn't know if she had the words. The first time he showed her the finished painting, she hadn't been able to speak. Later she would tell Harry that she just didn't *get* art, but she didn't need a PhD to know how Elliot's work made her feel.

"It's me," she said finally, almost surprised.

He laughed nervously. "Well, yes. I paint what I see."

"No, I mean—it's *me*. That's what I look like."

He laughed again but didn't say anything. She didn't bother trying to explain that she was surprised at how beautiful she looked. He hadn't gone out of his way to flatter her with this portrayal; it wasn't as if she suddenly had fuller breasts and redder lips. But he had looked at her, and he had seen, and he had found every beautiful thing about her and put it on the canvas. No one had ever looked at her that way before.

Harry was already in the next gallery, whose muted gray walls set off the fantastic colors in the paintings. A placard labeled this as his Rainbow Period. This work was from much later in his life; she was relatively confident her painting would not be in this room.

Then again, she wasn't sure she would be able to find herself in her painting at all. By the time she met Harry, so many years ago, she had already made herself unrecognizable. Harry never knew the woman Elliot painted. The burnished red tangles of hair had been cropped short in anger and dyed a sensible businesswoman brown. Now, almost fifty, she was entirely transformed. She had fat on her hips and stretch marks on her stomach from bearing three children. Her breasts were starting to sag. There were lines on her face, creases of age and worry and heartbreak. And her eyes looked so tired. She wondered if, given the chance, Elliot would be able to find anything beautiful in her now.

She hadn't just enjoyed feeling attractive, though. Sometimes she stayed after her clothes were back on and the paint was drying on the canvas. She washed his paintbrushes and made him explain the mysterious tools in his drawing desk. She learned the difference between 9B and 7H graphite. He taught her how to keep perspective drawings in proportion by judging lengths based on a pencil held at arm's length. Sometimes he'd put on a pot of coffee and they would sit together at his kitchen table, talking and listening to the machine percolate. She laughed at the contents of his refrigerator (alcohol, ketchup, peanut butter) and when she learned that sometimes he ate nothing but Ramen for weeks so he could afford paint supplies, she took to bringing him bags of fresh fruit from the stand near her apartment. Cherries, peaches, strawberries—even years later she still associated these tastes with that summer. He told her he would have to take up still-life.

She understood now the intensity of his stare, though it had unnerved her at first. It wasn't just the striking green of his eyes; it was the way he looked at her, even when they were just discussing the heat wave or how much she hated waitressing. He always held her gaze a moment too long, until she could feel her face flush. But this behavior was beginning to make sense, because she found herself noticing things in her world that she had missed before. The particularly beautiful filigree shadow a wrought-iron balustrade threw on the sidewalk. The symmetry of two sisters sitting in the sandbox at the park playground, their heads bowed together over a lumpy castle. The way light caught in the folds of an old woman's shawl as she stepped on the escalator at a subway station. Of course. Once you paid attention, you realized there was so much to see.

Even with her newfound understanding, she still teased Elliot for his obsession with detail. He made her adjust her poses down to where her eyelashes brushed her cheek. Knee here, elbow there. Tuck the ankle. Fingers relaxed. However obedient her limbs were, her hair was ever tormenting him—the light coming in from the window made her hair glow too brightly; on humid days she sported a fuzzy halo of red frizz. One afternoon he had her spiral a curl around her finger until it would drape properly over her shoulder.

"Wanton ringlets," he said, coming close enough that she could feel the warmth of his breath on her collarbone.

"What?" she asked, shifting forward onto her elbows.

"Nothing," he said, stepping back. "It's Milton, from Paradise Lost. Lean back again, please."

She looked it up later. It took her almost three hours holed up in the public library to discover the singular phrase, but she found it. It was how Adam described Eve when they were together in Paradise, naked and shameless.

There were other paintings in his studio. Landscapes, some abstract pieces. But the ones she paid attention to were the portraits. Specifically the study of another young woman, the same green couch. Dahlia wasn't sure what to think. She felt a twinge of something like jealousy.

"Who's that?" she asked once when she was feeling bold. Her clothes were back on and Elliot was washing brushes in the deep paint sink by the window.

"Helen," he said without looking up.

She leaned in close until Helen's face blurred into peach smudges, her hair a slash of burnt umber.

"She's pretty," Dahlia said. She watched Elliot's shoulders shrug. "Don't you think so?" she pressed. She stepped back again, trying to look at the painting objectively. Helen had a high forehead and her hair curled into little tendrils by her ears. Dahlia noted with some consternation that Helen also had very full breasts with perfectly symmetrical nipples.

"I don't really think of it in terms of beauty," Elliot said now, shutting off the faucet. He turned around and leaned against the sink, considering the painting. "I just like to see things and put them on the canvas. If you start adding beauty into the equation, you miss what's really there. I don't want to cloud my judgment."

"Oh, come on," Dahlia said, teasing now. "You didn't think she was the least bit pretty?"

He rolled his eyes. She grinned and turned back to the canvas, making kissing noises and pretending to moon over the painted face. "What, you didn't have a little bitty crush on her?"

"Please," Elliot scoffed. "I can't let myself get distracted like that."

Her smile must have faltered, because his frown softened suddenly. "It's nothing personal, of course," he said. "It's just, you can't look at the world like that if you want to be an artist. At least if you want to be a good one."

Dahlia dropped her hand from the canvas. "Look at the world like how?"

He looked away from her and back to the painting, as if he were trying to catch Helen's attention.

"There isn't room for that kind of attachment in what I do," he explained. "Things like attraction. Or love. It muddles your vision. Stops you from seeing clearly."

Then he went back to scrubbing paint off his hands. Dahlia stayed in front of the painting for a long time, looking at Helen and wondering if she had ever sipped coffee from one of Elliot's blue-glazed mugs. She decided that Helen had not.

Harry never spoke of love like this, as if it were an obstacle. Even when he admitted that the thought of her distracted him from grading papers and made him forget what he was talking about in the middle of his lectures, he said it with gleeful acceptance. The first time he told Dahlia he loved her, his hands were shaking and he confessed that he'd been wanting to say it since their second date. They were sitting in a restaurant together, celebrating their two month anniversary. She looked down at her bitten fingernails and wished, fleetingly, that for Harry's sake she were another woman. But then he was looking at her with such hope and terror that she had to still his trembling hands and say, "I love you, too." It wasn't a lie, which surprised her. She thought of the way his body curved protectively around hers in the darkness when she slept over at his place, how he called her to say goodnight when they were apart. He made her laugh while she waited for her clothes to spin dry at the laundromat. He knew that she liked her movie popcorn with no butter, extra salt. It wasn't wrong to tell him she loved him. It just gave her an odd sensation in her limbs, like the spaces between her bones were too small. An unsettled feeling that took a long time to fade, even when they were back in his apartment and Harry was whispering his nicknames for her in her ear. "Marigold. Tulip. Tigerlily. Chrysanthemum." A whole bouquet. "Dahlia, Dahlia, Dahlia."

Elliot called her Doll. It was an accident at first, Dahl, a call not fully formed. But it stuck, because she was his life-size doll and posed the way he wanted.

"I love painting you," he said once. His voice was low, as if this were a confession. Then he stood up straighter, cleared his throat. "I think it's your hair. I've never seen that color red before. I would need to paint it a thousand more times to get it right."

Their eyes met over the canvas and for the first time in her posing experience she felt trapped. She wanted more than anything to get off the damn couch and go to him, but she couldn't, because the shadows playing off her hands were perfect the way they were. She was a butterfly, pinned to a card, when all she wanted was to flutter around his light, to dust his eyelashes with the iridescence of her wings.

She shifted her pinky a millimeter to the left.

"Hold still, Doll," he reminded her.

She longed to tell him certain things. Things like how she loved the smell of asphalt during a September rain, but not as much as she loved the whiff of turpentine that lingered in the air when he passed by her. How she'd learned the names of all the colors he painted with. Cadmium yellow, alizarin crimson, titanium white, burnt sienna, pthalo green. How she whispered his name like a prayer every night before she fell asleep.

While he painted she thought about making love to him. One of his cracked-paint hands reaching out for her, not to arrange her limbs or brush hair out of her eyes, but to touch her, to pull her over to the mattress with its wrinkled navy blue sheets. She thought about him streaking a line of ultramarine blue down the valley between her breasts, circling her navel with his thumb. Pressing a cadmium red palm to her heart. Connecting her freckles with naples yellow. She could almost imagine how it would feel, the cool paint slicked onto her skin. Elliot kissing her ribs until the paint dried, until his lips were blue and red and yellow. The bed beneath them might look like a Pollock, or a kindergartener's finger painting.

All this while he painted only ten feet away. It was too close and the farthest of distances. She didn't know how to be this way, how to want two completely different things at the same time. She wanted him to put down the brush and kneel by the couch and kiss her hard on the mouth. She wanted him to stay exactly where he was and never come a step closer.

She was good at loving from afar. Pining for her favorite singer on the radio, taking comfort in the miles of crackling static and airwaves between them. Developing a tremendously inappropriate crush on her young, 20-something pastor from the safe distance of her church pew. Flirting with her childhood best friend, Jack, who was tall and cute and as gay as they come. She relished the safety of impossible love the way some might relish a perfect kiss.

But love that smelled of turpentine and stared at her with bottle glass eyes, love that knew the particular constellation of freckles on the small of her back, love that wanted to paint her hair a thousand times just to get it right—this kind of love terrified her. She could only think in fragments. Verbs escaped her when she was in his presence, conjunctions quivered on her tongue, nouns would not be released. She had to remind herself to exhale, otherwise she might keep sucking in breath after breath until her lungs burst. She had not known it was possible to need something so badly.

Harry was still talking, but she couldn't focus on what he was saying. They were getting close to her painting, she could feel it. She wondered if Harry would be able to figure out, in spite of all the red hair and slenderness, that the subject of the painting was her.

She doubted it. When Harry looked at her, she never felt naked. Even when he watched her undress. No one but Elliot ever made her feel truly naked, all the layers of flesh and slippery muscle stripped away. Years later she still had the same dream: she was reclining on the green couch and Elliot was painting her. When she looked down at her hands, she realized she was only a skeleton.

Harry was crossing the gray room when she saw it through the arched doorway into the next gallery. A five by three foot oil painting of a nude woman sprawled on a bare mattress. She did not recognize the woman, but Dahlia knew her painting would be in this room, too.

"Go ahead," she told Harry. "I'll be right back. I just want to look at something."

This wasn't entirely true. She didn't *want* to look. She needed to, in order to put this whole thing to rest. She had not gone to Elliot's funeral. This museum visit was her eulogy to him.

She locked her eyes on the floor and edged into the room that held her painting, terrified that she might catch sight of herself before she was ready. She moved along the edge of the room, reading the title cards of each piece. *Reclining Nude. Nude Woman at the Window. Nude Woman, Seated. Woman Sleeping.* She did not know the name of her painting, but she thought she might know when she saw it.

And then she found it. *Doll, Naked.* Of course.

She closed her eyes and backed up a few steps before realizing that she could not do this all at once. This was not just any of the series of nude studies he had done of her. This was the final painting, the one she had never seen. The one he must have completed from memory, after she disappeared from his life. Her hands hovered in front of her face and she was briefly reminded of her younger self, watching through her fingers in the movie theater while a horror film flashed on the screen in front of her. As if seeing slivers of the gore might calm her racing heart or assuage her nightmares later that night.

Planting herself squarely on both feet, she spread her hands so just one eye could peek out. She squinted until the brushstrokes of the painting dulled into an Impressionist blur. With the piece looking like this, fragmented by her fingers and softened by her hazy eyes, she could almost fool herself into dropping her hands and looking at it dead on. But she knew that such a decision might send her reeling backwards, out of this gallery, out of the museum, out of the city. So she waited. She let her eyes focus again, still mostly shielded by her hands. She breathed. It felt rather like approaching Medusa, what with the way she was so braced against seeing.

But no death rattle emanated from the painting, no coiled snakes hissed at her. It was, after all, just pigment on a canvas. Someone's 25-year-old brushstrokes, a heavy wooden frame. No danger. She slid her hands further down her face, off her eyes, and blinked to clear her vision.

Ah. So. There it was, no longer filtered through her fingers or squinted eyes. The painting as it was meant to be seen. She took a deep, steadying breath. The swirling feeling in her stomach reminded her of the first time she had ridden a bike. There was exultant joy in the moment, flying down the sidewalk on two wheels. But the second she remembered the impossibility of such a balancing act, the sidewalk careened toward her, the horizon tilting.

She tried to stop thinking, just for a moment. Tried to see the painting as if it were the portrait of a stranger, as if it had not been painted by a man she loved fiercely.

A young, redheaded woman stood in a dark room. Moonlight poured over her in a stream from the skylight overhead. Her hands were on her hips and she was not smiling. The set of her lips suggested she was holding her breath, holding herself together. Her eyes were bright and wet-looking.

Dahlia swallowed hard. None of this should matter anymore. She was a different woman now. She had a husband and children and dust in her house. Twenty-five years ago may as well have been a million.

But the memory was crystallized in her mind. It was December. Elliot had forgotten to turn up the heat and Dahlia sat shivering on the couch, her nipples puckered into hard peaks. He had offered her tea, but she said scotch and soda would warm her up faster. He took the hint.

She watched while he squeezed a dab of red onto the palette and swirled his brush through it. She took another sip of the scotch and held it in her mouth until her tongue burned. It wasn't helping at all. The back of her throat ached. Couldn't he tell she was miserable? Her shivering grew violent, and maybe it knocked something loose inside her.

"Elliot."

He looked up, startled. She never spoke once they began working. "Yes?"

She shook her head. The words were stuck at the back of her mouth. She could feel them there, rolling like marbles on the back of her tongue, but she did not know how to spit them out. Her eyes prickled. Elliot looked at her with his sea glass eyes and took a step forward. Then another.

Then he was so close she could feel the heat of his body; it made the molecules in the air vibrate faster. She sat very still. His hand hovered near her face. They were both holding their breath. It was so quiet she could hear the soda water fizzing, the bubbles hurling themselves into the air, breaking the surface like little sighs. If he would just shift a millimeter forward—

He pulled his hand back and gestured to his forehead.

"Your hair's in your eyes," he said. He went back to the canvas.

She felt her stomach turn over. She was starving. She had been waiting for him to throw anything her way, a scrap of affection, the most meager of bones, and he had failed her. She was shaking not with cold but with rage now, the kind of terrible anger only young people in love can harbor.

"Please," she said. She wished her voice did not come out so cracked and desperate. "Please just tell me the truth."

She was at the edge of the precipice, teetering. A rush of energy flooded her limbs, the same energy she felt the first time she stepped out of her clothing in his apartment, reborn. There was something exhilarating about the truth. She jumped.

"Please tell me you have feelings for me, too."

He turned back to face her very slowly. His eyes were different; unfocused. He was seeing something else.

"I'm sorry, Dahlia." He pronounced her name deliberately.

Dahlia understood it then. The peculiar danger of falling in love with someone was that you gave them exactly the words to break you.

"I never meant to give you the wrong impression."

She stood up. "Please, Elliot. Give me something. Tell me it's not just me."

The silence roared in her ears.

"But you—you kept asking me to come back! You wanted to paint me!"

"I hired you."

The words were steel. She sputtered unintelligibly for a moment, trying to formulate the right logic to convince him that he was wrong. What she meant to say was *I let you see inside me.* Nothing came out.

"I'm sorry," he said. He held out the robe to her.

"No," she said. "We have a session to finish."

She threw the robe on the floor and went back to the couch but did not sit. She hated him then. Her knuckles were burning. She put her hands on her hips and faced him, her mouth set in a line.

"Go ahead," she said. "Paint me. Hurry up, I'm being paid by the hour."

"Dahlia—"

"*Paint me.*"

The haze cleared from the bottle green eyes and he picked up the palette. She made eye contact with him and saw him wince. Good. He bent his head over the paints. Her eyes stung with concentration. *Look at me*, she thought. *Look at me.*

Her eyes were stinging again as she stood in front of the painting. She heard a familiar cadence of footsteps behind her.

"Oh," Harry said.

It was more of an exhalation than a word, the sighing of air from his lungs. Dahlia could feel the weight of his breath on the back of her neck and she knew something sad had broken open inside him. It was a different type of ache from her own, but she could feel it just the same. The terrible realization that certain beauty will always be out of our grasp.

Sweet, brilliant, clueless Harry. He could talk about perspective and vanishing points and oil on canvas for hours without ever putting brush to paper. He did not create things. She tried very hard not to pity him because of that.

Harry loved her, he really did. He strived for her happiness. Years ago he had noticed how often she visited museums, how frequently she ducked into dinky, one-room galleries they passed on their afternoon walks. He thought it was a love of art. He didn't know she was looking for something.

After two years together, he proposed to her in the Met. It was January and the cold winter light sunk through the panes of the enormous glass wall where the Temple of Dendur was housed, coloring everything sallow and gray. Harry had insisted they come early on a Sunday morning when the museum was almost empty. Their footsteps echoed in the quiet, and Dahlia could see her reflection in the dark water that surrounded the temple. The surface was so still that she could also see the flash of terror in her eyes when Harry tugged her hand and knelt, fumbling with a velvet box.

She knew already what her answer would be, but as she felt the word drop from her lips into his waiting hands, she was thinking that this couldn't have felt more wrong. The Temple of Dendur was dedicated to Isis and Osiris. Lovers who saved each other. Isis gathered the pieces of her husband when he was broken and breathed life into him. How could

Dahlia be expected to hold Harry together when she couldn't even find all the pieces of herself?

She had said yes to him anyway. Because she could form coherent sentences around him, and because she was lonely and thought he could fix that. His hands were gentle. His eyes reminded her of the basset hound she'd had as a child. But even though she knew he couldn't possibly hurt her the way Elliot had, she was so much more careful with Harry. She doled out little spoonfuls of herself. If he noticed her stinginess, he didn't say anything. He accepted these offerings and celebrated them.

And she was grateful for him. He could love her the way she needed to be loved, and that had saved her. It was enough. Enough that she could marry him and have three beautiful children and be happy most of the time.

It was only sometimes that she woke up in the middle of the night and found herself unable to fall asleep again. She'd see the knobs of Harry's spine illuminated in the green glow of the alarm clock, the rise and fall of his breathing, and that old unsettled feeling would creep into her bones until she had to leave the apartment, walk down the block, turn at the Asian grocery store on the corner, and keep going until she saw the letters appear, the familiar alphabet soup that meant escape. N, R, Z, W. A, B, C. The escalator would draw her down into the yellow-lit, weatherless underworld of the subway where she could swipe her MetroCard and ride until the knots in her stomach loosened and her heartbeat slowed.

Most of the time she felt better. The feeling would pass and she could get off at the next station, take a cab home and climb into bed without Harry noticing her absence. Except sometimes she caught her reflection in the darkened window and watched it hover there until the train coasted into the next station and she disappeared. Then she saw Elliot in each window of the subway car, like snapshots in a photo album of the life she might have had. Sometimes bearded, sometimes clean-shaven, always slightly out of view so she could never tell for certain if it was him. Sometimes a woman was clinging to his hand, other times a child, and sometimes he was alone, hands tucked in his pockets as he waited on the platform for the next train. It didn't matter. A taste like panic clawed at the back of her throat and she would have to remind herself to breathe. But then the doors would whoosh closed, sealing her in again. The train would lurch slightly, throwing her off balance, and the velocity would hurl her onward once again.

"This is something, Dahlia. I mean—"

Harry's sentence broke off. The professorial authority had evaporated. A long silence hung between them. When he spoke again his voice was tight, wrapped around a thin wire of grief.

"She's beautiful."

Dahlia could not speak.

"You know," he said suddenly, "she looks like you."

Dahlia shook her head. "I'm old and fat."

Harry touched her wrist. "No, you're not. But that's not what I mean. Look, there, the shape of her lips. That's exactly the face you make when you're upset with one of the kids. Like you're angry but you could just burst out laughing any second."

Without looking at him, she cleared her throat. "Explain it to me."

Out of the corner of her eye, she could see him studying the painting, as if trying to remember something long since forgotten.

"Well," he said. "Gregory's a genius. In one painting you can see an entire story. The woman…it's not the first time she's done this, but she's not an experienced model. See the way she's got her hands on her hips? It's like she's trying to put up a brave front, but look at her fingers. She's holding on for dear life. She's terrified. Ashamed."

Dahlia nodded, remembering. Harry took a step closer, his gaze fixed on the painting.

"But then look at her mouth, her forehead. She's resolute, almost defiant in her nakedness. She's not trying to hide. And her eyes."

He leaned forward, his expression soft, the crease between his brows smoothing. "It's what Gregory did best. You know exactly what she's feeling."

"Do you?"

"Oh, yes. Look at her. The simultaneous terror and joy, the terrible need. She was in love with Gregory."

Dahlia closed her eyes.

"But it's more than that," Harry continued. Dahlia's eyes opened. "The brushstrokes on this woman are different than all the others. Gregory usually painted so furiously he slopped the paint onto the canvas and then smeared it into place. But not here. See? He used a tiny brush for her face. It's delicate. And the thinness of the paint on the rest of her body suggests a very slow, very deliberate method. Even the way the light frames her is different. The moonlight just spills in from overhead and pools on the floor. Look at the way it halos her face. It's like he didn't need to light her because her beauty was enough on its own."

Dahlia blinked away the sting from behind her eyes. "And what is all of that supposed to mean?"

Harry turned back to face her, his eyes shining. He smiled at her, a hard kind of smile. "Gregory was in love with her, too."

So Elliot had loved her. Elliot M. Gregory. Twenty-five years later and she still didn't know what the M stood for. Dahlia turned away from the painting. She looked at her husband, and he looked back at her. She thought maybe he saw something.

Ryan Stone

Tying Up the Replacement

Albert hated the Yorkshire Terrier, the Yorkie. Such a detestable name for a breed. It sounded like some swank neighborhood outside some Northeastern, trash-ridden city. Yorkshire. Yorktown. Yorkieville. Its stump legs wiggled under it even when he lifted it up onto the bed next to his wife, Anna. It never seemed to stop moving and twitched when it slept. The thing made him nervous. He thought it might twitch its way into his collectible cabinet where his antique plates were displayed and wreak a havoc he couldn't fathom. He rushed home each day from his tidy law office on the square in downtown Harrison with the vision of the dog sitting amidst his beautiful blue plates, the pieces of glass shattered and strewn about like bits of his soul. The dog's smug little face twitching at him. It was almost more than he could bear, but he loved his wife, and she loved the dog, and each day he slouched out the front door and took the dog for a walk around the neighborhood so that, as she put it, he could be a good dog owner.

"You've never done anything *for* anything else, Albert," she said from the bed. "You should have to take care of at least one thing in your life."

"I'm taking care of you," he said. He leaned down and stroked her gray hair. Her hair that had been a beautiful brown with natural reddish highlights only a few months before. The stress of dying pressed on them with a weight that forced the air out of their lungs. "Besides, that's not true. What about raising Micala? What about her?"

"Something of less stature," she said. "It will humble you."

He didn't feel humbled. He felt obligated to something that needed him. He disliked being needed by lesser things. He saw it in his clients who whined about their declining disability checks, who were caught carrying a sofa with a reported slipped disc. There existed an unlimited line of whiners that stretched out of Harrison, down Route 12 to Donovan, onto the Interstate, and around the globe. He hated whiners. The dog was particularly adept at whining, especially in the morning before he was fully awake. His daughter never whined, not even when she was a child. After she graduated from law school, he traveled to the West Coast to visit her. He went alone, surfing along the great expansive stretches of highway in Kansas and Colorado, barreling on through. He barely noticed the Rockies as his old Chevy churned up their slopes, arching downward with sudden, steep plunges. When he got to California, he didn't stop to look at the massive redwoods or admire the way the waves exploded against the Pacific shoreline. He went straight to his daughter's apartment, knocked on the door, and smiled, extended the flowers he'd bought at a florist not three blocks away. She hugged him when she recovered from the shock. She was so different than he remembered her. So angled. Her face had crevices. Etches spread from her exhausted eyes. So different from her former softer self with her round and small face, her eyes bright, her hair lifting gently in the wind. Now, she had cropped it short, so she could study, she said, instead of do anything to her hair. Law school did such things to people, he knew. He'd been through it himself, but he had hoped it wouldn't change her. Of course, he'd hoped in vain. Most things he'd hoped for about her were entirely in vain.

He took the dog for its walk each morning. The thing looked so inauspicious at the end of the leash, as if a bird of prey could sweep down and find itself a nice morsel to nibble on. There were plenty of other people who walked their dogs early in the morning, though some of them simply opened the door and let the dog run into the street. He found, shortly after he started the morning walk, that he enjoyed it. He liked the time alone. The sting of the early-morning air. The control he had over the little dog trotting along next to him. It was a good time to think, and the air outside didn't smell like the air inside his house. Outside it smelled fresh and promising. On the walk, he would feel as if something good may happen to him some day, and he would think about the possibilities and tromp along through snow and wind and, sometimes, rain. He never missed a day for the twenty minute excursion, and the dog came to expect it so that when he felt the dog's tongue on his cheek in the morning, it wasn't so bad. He had something to get up for.

It was particularly crisp on the first morning the dog got away from him. The air smelled of curing leaves and dirt, the deep smells of autumn.

Someone's bar-b-que already in use sent wafts of searing meat to his nose. The dog smelled it, too, and in a moment of rather deep reflection on Albert's part, simply slipped away. He didn't notice it at first. His thoughts were on his daughter and how she might be doing in Kansas City. He'd heard she took a new job with a different law firm and hoped to stay on until she made partner. So much more vibrant than he was, so much more driven. She had clerked for him, in a way, while she was still in high school. She prepared briefs for him. She wrote his closing arguments a few times. He never told anyone because it was slightly unethical, though only slightly. But she was good. So good. She went to Stanford and received offers from firms in D.C. and New York, but she wanted to be close to home, so she came to Kansas City, only five hours away, and quickly got a job with a small firm. She was a star there, a big fish in a medium pond. He was proud of her as he thought of her bent over the worn and simple oak table in the front room of his office, studying law books, reading everything, digesting so much more than he ever had. He had books on his shelves he'd never even touched. She read them all, brought them to him. *Let's discuss this case, Daddy*. He'd look at the book, realize he'd never touched it, and tell her he was too busy right now. She was twelve then, still a child, but he saw her in such a different way, so mature and polished. Not like him. Not like her mother either. No life in her eyes. And now, she was a corporate attorney with the stereotypical heart of ice. She told him on the phone once how she could freeze a jury with her eyes. *All I have to do is look at them*, she said, *and they know I'm right*. He was remembering the conversation and what he had said in reply and what he had asked when he noticed he was no longer holding the leash and the Yorkie had vanished.

He searched for an hour, calling the dog's name, calling its nickname, offering a treat. A num-num. His wife had decided to call a treat a num-num. He felt ridiculous. The town defense attorney, the one who took on tough cases for the under-paid, wandering the park calling out for an offensively small dog, yelling out, "Do you want a num-num?" He was sure people stared at him out their windows. *Did you see Albert Gilbert out there this morning? What a sight that was*. What a sight indeed. He went down a small hillside that dipped off a path that circled the park. A line of houses backed up to the hillside, their fences just at the bottom. He shaded his eyes and peered up and down the fence. Seven houses down, he saw wisps of smoke and smelled the bar-b-que. At the back fence's base sat the Yorkie apparently obediently awaiting a far better num-num. The dog sat unusually still, only moving to lift its nose to the air. He went over, picked the dog up, and carried it the whole way home. His morning walk was ruined, his thoughts broken. He couldn't even remember what he was going to tell Anna when he got back. Something about their daughter. He was flustered.

At home, Anna asked him how the walk went. He didn't answer her at first, just set the dog down on the kitchen floor and stood there looking at it. He hated the thing's devilish ears, its puffy tail, its long hair that dangled from its chin like some Chinese Zen master perched in the lotus position atop a distant peak. The little dog, in all his estimation, was ugly. Anna called again from the bedroom, asking about the walk. Usually, he came back with something to talk about, some little tidbit he had dreamed up on his walk about a vacation they could take together or a new dish he wanted to try or some brave-new-world political idea. They would sit for an hour or so before he had to go into the office and discuss his idea. It began to seem that it was all that kept her alive, the moment of possibility when they would yammer on about traveling off the Greek coast, lounging on a yacht's deck in sun chairs, bathing each other in dark tanning oil, sipping Ouzo and feeding each other olives. She called for him again, this time only his name in the form of a question.

"I'm here," he said. He shook his head a little.

"How was the walk?"

"I lost something," he said.

"What?"

"I'm not sure," he said. He went to the bathroom and washed his face with cold water. Inside, he felt unsure of what to say to his dying wife when he went to the bedroom. He couldn't tell her the dog got away. Of that he was sure. Even though he found the dog, he knew she would make him cease the walks, and there would be no coming back from that. He dried his face and his thick eyebrows and went back to the kitchen.

"Aren't you coming in here?" Anna called.

"Just a minute," he said. He got out a tray and placed two coffee cups opposite one another. He filled them with cold coffee from the pot, then placed them in the microwave for four minutes. He listened to the hum. For some reason, the dog, who usually bounced around and would be up in the bed with Anna by now, had not left its spot where it sat on the kitchen floor.

"Where's Francie?" Anna called.

Francie. A ridiculous name for anything, even a dog such as the one that sat just a foot away from him.

"He's in here with me," he called back. He leaned down. "It appears we need one another," he said in a low voice. "Not a word on what happened today." He pointed at the dog. "You got it? Not a word."

When his daughter was young, they shared secrets from Anna. Little things like going to Dairy Queen and eating ice cream or the packet of gum he would buy her at the IGA. The truth was Anna would not have minded, but it felt special, something to hold onto between them. When she was a little older, he tried to share things with her about himself, things he prided himself on like his work ethic and his charisma with a jury. She laughed at him, giggled at him when she was thirteen. She told her friends that her father was a blowhard. So, he stopped, and ever since had felt a little valley inside himself, dug out by her little giggles, until she passed the bar, got the job in Kansas City. At first, she called him almost every night to tell him what was new at the firm. New cases they had in the pipeline. New clients. Everything was new to her then and worth sharing. Office politics. The grind of working. He told her his experience, told her how when he was a young law clerk things were different, things moved so much slower. He told her he could hardly keep up.

She called less and less as the years went on, and now, she never called. Never visited except around the holidays. She was engaged. They barely knew the boy. Man. He thought of the fiancé as a boy. She brought him with her to Christmas not long after Anna was diagnosed. It was before they had told their only daughter about the illness. The boy had long, shiny hair and worked in the theater industry. He was a lighting specialist. He lit things just right, and while they sat around their little dining room table, chewing on Anna's perfectly-cooked turkey and wonderful dressing, he commented on how the lighting in the room could be altered and arranged so that it would highlight the room's prevalent features, like the dark-stained chair rail that ran around the room and the Renoir print that hung just behind Anna's head. The boy said it needed to be lit up so that it shined like a movie star. Shed some light on things, he said. It's the only way to go.

They left right after dinner, and his daughter had only come back three or four times since, always by herself but always still engaged to the light boy. The wedding loomed somewhere in the future and, at times, he wondered if they had actually eloped.

The dog pulled harder the next morning, but his focus was entirely on maintaining control. He tried to think but nothing came to him. He found his mind blank and bored with the damp, gray morning. Everything around him seemed as if he'd fallen off the planet into a netherworld of dried up life. The little dog pulled again, and he yanked back on the leash. The thing let out a yelp.

"I'm sorry," he said, bending over to pet the dog. "Are you okay?" His hand came up and found the dog's collar, and he unsnapped the leash. The little thing knew immediately that it was free and it bolted away from him on its stumpy legs. Its hair flew wildly as Francie bounded across the open field in the middle of the park. Halfway across, the dog stopped and turned back to stare at him. He waved at it.

"Go on," he shouted.

The dog turned and ran toward the other side of the park, and he took off after it at a lazy trot, hoping it would stay out of the road.

A week later, he came home from the walk and went to the bedroom with a bounce in his step. Anna was not in the bed. She was not in the room. He called for her down the little hallway that led to their daughter's old room. Before he entered the room, he knew she was in there. She sat at the window, staring out into the magnolia tree in the tiny side yard. The limbs stretched over the fence into the neighbors yard, and every year, in the spring, the tree blossomed and dropped fragile pink flowers on both sides of the fence like some kind of peace offering.

"What's wrong?" he asked.

"Melvina Harris called," she said. She didn't look at him. "She said she saw our dog running in the street. She said you were letting it go and that I should talk to you about it because there's a leash law, don't I know."

He sighed and sat down on the bed. No use denying it. Melvina Harris never called anyone except to complain about things she had a right to complain about.

"What are you trying to do to me, Harold?" She touched her face, held her hand flat against her cheek. "I love that dog."

"I know," he said. "Fine. I'll keep him on the leash from now on."

"I want you to stop taking him for walks," she said.

"Why?"

"I've been thinking about Micala," she said. "She's up there in the city where they have better hospitals. I think we should move there."

"Move there?"

"Yes," she said. "I think it would be best for both of us. We'd see her again. We'd be a part of her life."

He thought for a moment of his daughter in the room as a very young child. She would run around the room in circles until she became dizzy and fall on the bed to let the whole world spin and spin, she said. *Daddy, stand above me so I can watch you spin.* The thought of trying to reenter her life in some meaningful way made his head hurt.

"I think I need this," she said. "I know I'm asking a lot."

"You are," he said. "There's a lot you're asking. Much more than I can give."

She stared at him for a moment before turning away. Her face looked blanched in the sun. He had to get to the office, he said, and turned to leave.

"Albert," she called after him. "The dog wants out."

The boxes lay strewn about the kitchen and living room. The bedroom was already packed. Micala and the boy had come to help, and they were in Micala's old room packing up dusty, moth-bitten clothing.

"You should just throw this stuff out, Dad," Micala said from the closet. "Mom wouldn't have minded."

"Keep it," he said. He stood in the doorway watching her move from the closet to the bed, tossing the clothing in a heap as she used to do when she was a teenager, working through what to wear everyday, tying her hair up in all kinds of confusing ways. He wanted to tell her he was sorry that he didn't know anything about raising children. Sorry that all he'd been for her was a spinning head, a library of law books.

"You okay, Dad?" she asked. Genuine concern in her voice, in the tone of it. But she was who she was, a good faker, by her own admission. He was never sure what to believe from her anymore.

"Sure," he said. "It's just a lot, you know?"

"This place in the city is great," she said. "And it's only forty minutes from our apartment. I'll visit every day, Dad." She came over to him and put her hand on his arm. She rubbed it up and down. Part of him wondered if she wanted to be a mother. "I mean, they have a tennis court. Shuffle board. There's a golf course just across the road. It's like paradise. They even have an Olympic-sized swimming pool. Can you imagine that?"

"Sure," he said. "What about the dog?"

"There's a pet deposit. I think it's like four or five hundred. But, yeah, the dog can come. If you want, I mean."

"Is there a place to walk the dog?"

"Sure. There's a path."

"I mean, is there an open field where he could run around."

"Dad, it's the city. There's very little open anything. And you can't take a dog off the leash there. They'll fine you right into the ground. And if he ever bites someone, who knows what happens then. You'll end up in court." She tossed more clothes on the bed. "I mean the whole damn place is sue-happy."

"So there's no place to let him go?"

"We can take him out to the country once or twice a month if you want."

"Sure," he said.

The lighting boy came into the room. He held up a lamp from the front room.

"You know this is actual lead glass?" he said. "Do you still want this?"

"I think we bought that in Texas," Albert said.

"Can I have it? I mean, it would look great on a set I'm designing for a community theater group. It's a perfect period piece, and when you turn it on, the focus of the light is straight downward, so it doesn't give off any illumination to the sides whatsoever. I mean it's all about the leaded glass and the vibrant colors, plus the area around the lamp is lit but it's still dark, you know? I mean talk about ambiance."

"Take it," Albert said. "You're more excited about it than I ever was."

"Awesome," light boy said. He left the room.

"He's an idiot," Albert said.

"Knock it off," his daughter replied. "He's great once you get to know him. He just gets really excited about lights."

"Seems like he gets turned on."

"You're out of line, mister," she said. She was joking with him. And they laughed at each other.

The dust clung to everything and made them sneeze and sniffle as they carried the clothing out to the car and tossed it unfolded into the trunk. The lighting boy continued loading a few things into a U-Haul. The rest, they'd decided, would be sold in an estate sale. Albert had very little left. The old clothes in the trunk were a hodgepodge of Micala's from when she was young and Anna's from when they were first married. A variance of generational attitudes, from eighties punk rock pink to forties felt dresses, stuffed into the Chevy. Albert went back in the house and found his way to the little kitchen where he sat down at the Formica table. His blue antique plates were stacked in neat rows. Micala came in and sat across from him. She pushed the plates gently to make room for her elbows and slender piano-player hands. She'd abandoned lessons after two weeks, saying the playing made her head hurt. All that tinking and binking, she said, tink, bink, tink, bink, plunk, blunk. She told her parents this at the kitchen table, and she had pushed her plate back to make room for her bony elbows and slight hands. She folded her hands in front of her face and put her elbows down, which made the blue plates clink together like the sound of the highest piano key. Albert flinched.

"There's something else," she said. "We've set a date."

He sighed. "Fine time to tell me that," he said. "Less than a month after your mother's funeral."

"It's not good timing, I know. But it is what it is. I'm getting married. You can't imagine how it makes me feel that Mom isn't here."

"I can get an idea," he said, "because I feel the same way." He stood up. "I should get the dog."

The dog hadn't been on a walk in over a month. They purchased a long rope and a yard stake from the pet store, and now the Yorkie was tied up in the backyard, running in circles until it fell down exhausted. Surely, its little world spun. Sometimes, when it fell down to rest, Albert would go to the backyard and stand over the dog, staring down at it. It would look back up at him, gazing at his head with its tiny black eyes.

From the table, Micala said, "Well, I'm going to find something to put these plates in. I know you won't want to leave them."

Albert decided to stay at the table while she packed the plates to make sure they received proper treatment. The dog could wait. After Anna died, he had taken care of everything so carefully. Her funeral had been exactly as she had wanted it, right down to the gardenias and lace doilies on the coffee table. The plates would be the same. Everything would be handled the same way. It was the only thing he could think of to keep him sane, especially without his walk each day. Without the dog, it seemed pointless and trivial. A man alone, trudging down some concrete path, his feet heavy, his face old, with no purpose or reason except to wander in his own misery. At least, that's how others would see it from the windows of their relaxed and retired living arrangements. He put his hand to his face and felt his heated, sweating forehead.

The lighting boy came in the kitchen and sat down across from him.

"You'll like living in the city," he said. "There's so much to do. You'll have to come to a show. I mean, there's biking and trails to walk on. You can just walk for miles and miles and never see the same thing. And there's food. Food like you've never seen or eaten before. I ate octopus. I mean, octopus, the other day. Have you ever heard of such a thing? And there's concerts and bowling alleys and water parks. You would love the water park. The old people go in the wave pool and go up and down, up and down. It's like a geriatric ocean, but they say it's relaxing. Some of them fall asleep out there and they have to pull them out. But that won't be you. You're not that old, Dad. And there's shopping. So much shopping, and all indoors at malls. You can walk around and around the mall. People do that. It's filtered air."

"What did you say?" he asked.

"I said there's filtered air."

"No, about me not being one that falls asleep? What was it you called me?"

The boy paused. "I don't know," he said, though clearly he did.

"You're an idiot," Albert told him. He put his elbows on the table and let his head fall into his cupped hands. The plates clinked.

"Well, everyone's entitled to their opinion." He stood up and was on his way out when Micala came back with a big box. "Your Dad's not feeling well," lighting boy said and went out through the dining room to the living room where he slammed the front door.

"What's his deal?"

"He's an idiot," Albert said.

"Stop it. You two need to get along."

"Fine," he said. "That box is too big. We're not packing them all in that big old box."

"It'll be fine. We'll pack it with packing peanuts and wrap the plates in newspaper and towels."

"Not good enough," he said.

"Sure it is," she said, and she began packing the plates. Albert forced himself up, though his back ached, and went over to the window. He peered into the backyard, searching for the Yorkie, but he couldn't see Francie. Albert could only hear the little dog as his claws scraped up and down the chipped and peeling back steps. Francie yapped at the back door, wanting in.

Poetry

Kristine Ong Muslim

What the Boatman Sees

after Monte Dolack's "Midnight All A Glimmer" (2004)

He stops paddling when he reaches the deepest part of the lake. He feels the water currents underneath his flimsy boat. For once, he is lonely enough to hear the cold. The moon, he knows, will not last long. All afternoon, the fat radio has been singing about the end of the world, and soon his death will be better than those of the others in town. The slight curve of the evening is shaped like a giant axe striking the surface of the lake, and he is just inches to the left of this slashing axe that will fell the world.

Evolving

Intention is one wing.
The nest will always be
too distant from the ground—
      there is no going back
or up. Falling is our book
of nights, letters to cousins
written on someone else's fur.

Stories we sing
to each other shade
and creep around
the intricate margins, sometimes
infectious, sometimes running
      loose, all wildness
      and teeth. I am
      nine syllables
      from my knees
and I cannot do
what you do.

Ronald Wallace

Mumbo Jumbo

We were standing on the street corner,
our houses hard behind us in the snow,
and if we hadn't much to say, we could
always retreat to the safety of home.
It was a bit awkward; we were new
neighbors, so I told him about my poetry
(what little there was to know)
and he told me about his laboratory
research—how we would have the cure
for cancer, he said, in under twenty years.
He was pursuing every lead–radiation,
chemo, a voodoo woman in Haiti and
her curious potent herbs. I thought he
might be putting me on, but no, he said,
if mumbo jumbo works, then mumbo
jumbo. That was twenty years ago. And now
his wife is dead of a cancer diagnosed
just weeks ago. And what are we to do?
We're standing on the street corner,
shoveling snow, our houses hard behind us,
no one home. And he's still talking
science. And I'm still talking poetry.
Whatever mumbo jumbo gets us through.

Erin Elizabeth Smith

Index of the Midwest

A poem about bridges leads to the voice
of a man who I almost forgot
I slept with to a street I got lost on
to the pink slip of tongue
between a calico's teeth.
The industrial corn stretching
out into an endless factory
of gold, nights in the complex pool,
airport food courts, breaking in
a front porch like a ship. Beggar's purses
with feta and corn. Shot glasses
like church windows and afternoons
smoking Camel Lights. No coming
to peace. No leaf turning
on an ancient record player.
If only there had been an escape hatch
in August's shorn fields. One that falls
forever into a flat dark, the story
of a girl who is almost.

Erin Elizabeth Smith

The Way the Cold Attaches

There's just one more story I have
to tell you. In it, it's December
and I'm looking out a window,
the street wet with brown snow.
Your car is not pulling to my curb,
though with every leaf of movement
I think it might.

If only this wasn't
the story—instead, you
in a museum, looking for me,
me looking for you. Yet there
we find the other, and we know
that's not true. Is it,
instead, me getting out of your car
that last Thursday we're lovers?
When you waved, I didn't
know what you meant;
I'd written the sense
from your hands—those four
lined fingers, the pressing
pressing thumb.

I don't know how to live
here. The December trees are slight
beneath their coats, so achingly
cold. Maybe this is the story—
in the park this afternoon
the snow stretched across the field,

ice-bright. I watched the city
simmer on the other side,
and there in that place I knew
I was the only woman
and you were not
the only man.

Jenn Monroe

I Feel In Your Absence All Rain

Dali's frame looms stories above my inattention. I don't know what to do about the clocks, never did, so instead I make my heart malleable, float its shadow over our entire landscape, one part in, one part out. We dabble, brushstroke to brushstroke, do this and this and this, become something other, then do that and that and that until we evolve again. But you took all of yourself today, your thin ghost, and my parting breath.

Face Down Days

I have seen the weather grieve, seen
it tear a woman apart,

the ropes that bind her body
to the world snapping taut ends.

I know well the faces met
at funerals, the stares of the bereaved

taking, always taking, and the way
the lines of mourners seem to snake

into the past, constricting the moment
where you live, and the other does not.

I have seen myself in the mirror
unshaven, addressing no one

in the deadened days
which those who have survived

must one by one face down.
I am writing this to say:

I hope you die first.
If one of us is to sit on a faded porch of the future,

trying to remember the curve of a jaw, or the feel
of something soft on the lips, I want it to be me.

Christopher Tozier

Dry Tortugas

It seems odd now to hear that prisoners
sobbed uncontrollably at the news
that they were to be imprisoned here.
They must have been allowed to wander freely
about the palms, pillars, and coral sands
as their inability to escape the island was certain.
Surely the clear waters teemed more so even
than they teem now with sweet swimming flesh.
Surely from the parapet more dolphins leapt,
many rays flew, hurricanes throbbed
safely through cerulean and silver air.

But sob they did and it wasn't for the reason we cry now.
They sobbed for the long intervals between mail,
the drinking water always warm, always salted.
They sobbed for the regular tides of yellow fever
and the season of calenture.
Oh how the noddies flew in
to the edge of the world and left them there
to thirst and burn and wretch alone on this sparkling beach
clutched to some civilized scrap of memory.

And as we lay here, half in the water, half on the sand
I can think of nothing quite so opposite
yet so much the same as I try to forget that bill,
that appointment that must be remembered,
how we've grown so calmly apart,
the tire treads, the dentist, the time.

How the warm waves lap so softly now,
how cool the iced lemonade swallows.
I fold your thin hand into mine
after you fall asleep. I hold you
and let the sun inject its fever.
I let the prisoner die.

Greg Billingham

A Play on Existence

so that no one sees
you release the wind on the shoulders of mountains
and carry the starving minutes
to a land on its knees.

so that no one sees
I take the beginning of each laugh
to a place where shadows go on searching
for their earlier selves.

so that no one sees
they map even the wilderness of their bedrooms
through the dark wandering
with the dawn breaking over their bodies

though I guess we can't always pretend
the horses in the alley don't remind
the fields of their freedom.

Greg Billingham

The Impossibilities of Words

To observe a fire and its science of burning
like a conversation of movements
in shades of red and blue,

and I must still create in broken castles
with pens that dream the color of words
a sentence that is softer than the sea
to remember how the rain had fallen
into its boundless self without talent,
beginning as the night's dark dress
trailed upon the floor.

For then the slow drift of sleep cannot touch me,
though it may extinguish everything we created
with words, piled towards an unstable heaven—

where I think it must have been a candle
that taught you how to dance
as it mimicked a dry leaf in the wind
        free to go anywhere.

Jamie Thomas

Song of Saturday Mornings

Those were the whole milk days—
sugar-stacked, calcium-thick—sitting

Indian-style in front of the snowy TV screen,
the cold cereal days, the pre- cholesterol-counting

or soymilk in the Midwest days,
the days of no intolerance.

When I am woken now
by my own child

before the light is much light,
I'm thinking of the Batman & Robin days,

the drunk stork bringing the wrong baby days, the days
of "what super power would be coolest to possess,"

of simple, footed pajamas, of no socks lost
to that place where socks are lost to,

that exists just beyond
a place of anything quite knowable.

Days of no remote control, then
little sister as remote control,

days of no control, no need for it—
three channels, no cable,

tinfoil on the rabbit's ears—
gigantic wooden console days,

Trojan console TV transmitting
big kid jokes to my little kid brain,

the healthy joking tragedies
flitting somewhere just to the left and over

my head—The Hulk theme song hasn't made me cry yet,
Superman isn't too lonely in his Fortress of Solitude—

these mornings glowed and pulsed with not,
not having punched a clock,

not having loved or learned,
of not having spilled orange juice

on your parents' comforter, or spilled
your secrets to those unwilling to hear,

not having won much, or lost
or even desired to, long before

I ever thought to wonder why
the superheroes led such solitary, phone-booth lives.

Paul David Adkins

Epipen

The army issues atropine auto-injectors
to counter chemical attack.
You slap them in your thigh
with a clenched fist.

My daughter is allergic
to pine, pollen, bees.

We stash banana-size
epipen syringes
in all backpacks
before hiking.

We never know where
flowers will attack,
pine cones drop nearby
like grenades.

We fear this—

all nature
rising against us
like apple groves
en route to Oz,

and bees the size
of those hideous monkeys
swooping down
to lift our girl
beyond hearing or sight,
breathless.

Timothy Kercher

The Chat

Just last night, me on the couch,
him on the chair next to the fire,
God and I were discussing
my wife and the children
she carries. I asked him if before
the beginning of the world, before
all this making something
from nothing, if he felt different,

like if the pre-creation him were
somehow a different version
of who he was. And I could tell
the question made him uncomfortable
by the way he stirred his hot chocolate,
the way that dark liquid spun
like the vast night sky, the marshmallows
like stars, circling and melting,

and I waited on the couch
for some type of answer, but
those few awkward moments
seemed an eternity and I felt
myself slipping into another
version of me, every moment
my babies growing stronger,
bigger, and me slipping
into the father I'll be.

Ruth Foley

Resolutions

This year, I'll write a poem that does not feature you,
a Christmas poem where I don't talk about your loss
and how you won't come back—and how you never do.
This year, I'll write about the holly, carols, frost—

a Christmas poem where I don't talk about your loss.
Although it was December when we got the news,
this year I'll write about the holly, carols. Frost
can be a symbol of rebirth, since I refuse

(although it was December when we got the news)
to write about your death when I can use the white
to be a symbol of rebirth. And I refuse
to count the times I've cried my way through Silent Night,

to write about your death when I can use the white
instead—the sky is black enough when Christmas comes.
To count the times I've cried my way through Silent Night,
it seems like overkill this year. Perhaps I'll hum

instead. The sky is black enough. When Christmas comes,
I'll light a match *and* curse the dark, hang lighted strings
that seem like overkill. This year, perhaps I'll hum
while I make apple pies and wrap the gifts—something

to light a match and curse the dark. The lighted strings,
the chestnuts on an open fire, the drummer boy…
While I make apple pies and wrap the gifts, something
is bound to fill my mind with tidings—comfort, joy,

some chestnuts on an open fire, the drummer boy.
I will not think of opening the gifts you left
(it will not fill my mind with tidings, comfort, joy).
I will not call to Heaven. Heaven has grown deaf.

I will not think of opening the gifts you left,
and how you won't come back, and how you never do.
I will not call to Heaven. Heaven has grown deaf.
This year, I'll write a poem that does not feature you.

Essays

Angie Chuang

On the Other Side of the Wall

Entering an Afghan home, whether a modern compound in Kabul or a mud-brick house in a village with no running water or electricity, is like peeling an onion. First, a guest enters through an outer wall that shields its inhabitants from onlookers. The door in the outer wall leads into an open-air courtyard, in which the guest is inside the compound, but still outside of the house. The guest will be ushered into the most accessible room from the courtyard, usually the *saloon,* the sitting room for the men. It's not unusual in smaller houses for those rooms to double as bedrooms, the long, narrow floor cushions on which people sit for meals turning into beds at night. No matter the size of the house, one things remains true, however: the innermost rooms, the ones that can't be seen from the courtyard, are reserved for the women—particularly the unmarried women, who must be shielded from strange and prying eyes. This was also true of the kitchen, where the women often congregated. Even in less conservative families which didn't hide women away, few outsiders, and almost never male ones, are allowed in those rooms. Full-length curtains hung between rooms and entryways, to provide more privacy.

Purdah, the Hindu and Islamic term for keeping women hidden from men through separation and veiling, comes from the Hindi word for "curtain." In the 1950s, Prime Minister Mohammad Daoud had abolished *purdah* in Afghanistan in an effort to modernize, and the communists, though they assassinated him, kept the ban in the spirit of Soviet male-female equality. In the 1990s, the *mujahideen*—anti-Soviet resistance fighters who waged civil war—brought it back, and after that, the Taliban enforced *purdah* in its most extreme form. Nevertheless, in all but the most modern (wealthy) families some version of it was always practiced. Entering an Afghan room, through the curtain, literally lifted a veil into another, inner world.

"Everyone in the city lived in a compound, a yard surrounded by walls that divided the world into a public and a private realm," author and Afghan American Tamim Ansary recalled in his post-9/11 memoir, *West of Kabul, East of New York*. "Visitors never really knew us because they never saw the hidden world inside our compounds. Those who came from the West didn't even know our private universe existed, or that life inside it was warm and sweet. And in a way, we Afghans didn't know we had this realm either, because we didn't know it was possible not to have it."

Afghan home design reflects a society that was fiercely protective of its own, distrustful of outsiders—out of necessity, as the often-invaded but never-conquered nation had learned. But at the same time, the famed Afghan hospitality dictated that once you were let in past the walls, you were a guest and would be fiercely embraced, provided for, and protected as one of the family. This was particularly true of the Pashtun ethnic group, which operated by a tribal code of *Pashtunwali*.

Ironically, this was the code that compelled the leadership of the Taliban, Afghanistan's ruling regime, to protect Osama bin Laden, the exiled son of a Saudi construction magnate, after the September 11 attacks. Bin Laden was not one of them, but the Taliban considered him their guest. Like a sheriff in a Wild West cowboy movie, President Bush called for bin Laden "dead or alive," and warned the world's leaders that they were with us or against us in the manhunt. The Taliban would not think of breaking *Pashtunwali* and giving up their guest. So the sheriff's posse prepared to ride in.

It was during this time, in the weeks after the terrorist attacks, that I first met the Shirzais.[1] My work as a newspaper journalist in Portland, Oregon, had become a blur of horrific footage on the newsroom television, Anthrax scares (some prankster sent an envelope full of Tide detergent to our office, prompting an evacuation and lots of frayed nerves), and anti-Muslim incidents to report on. I did my job, but felt helpless as the America around me nursed a rapidly growing hunger for retaliation that brought a forgotten country into the spotlight—or crosshairs, as it were. President Bush threatened to bomb Afghanistan

---

[1] The first and last names of the family members and some place names have been changed to protect the safety of relatives in Afghanistan.

"back to the Stone Ages." Commentators and comedians retorted that the war- and famine-ravaged nation didn't have far to go. The War on Terror was about to begin. "Afghanistan," my editor said as he leaned over my waist-high cubicle wall. "Do you have any contacts with Afghan immigrants?"

"Umm, no," I said, embarrassed, as I flipped through a Rolodex of mostly Latino surnames—Andrade, Benavidez, Caceres. I had been convinced that Latin American immigration would be the story of the new millennium.

"We're looking for someone," he said, chewing on the end of his pen, "to put a human face on the country we're about to bomb."

I nodded, chewing on the meaning of his words.

"The higher-ups want you to drop everything you're doing and make this a priority," he said. "We're asking a photographer to accompany you full time on this. The photo department's going to free up Stephanie."

That was the first good news I had heard in a long time. Stephanie Yao was a friend, and my favorite photographer to work with. A fellow Chinese American, she had a quiet and sensitive demeanor that worked well with the kinds of stories I did—and balanced my considerably louder and more probing one. But I needed to find someone to photograph first. At a time when mosques were being attacked by hate mail and graffiti, and newly minted bumper stickers featured "Weather Forecast for Afghanistan: 13,500 degrees Fahrenheit" inscribed over a mushroom cloud, I correctly anticipated that it would be difficult to find Afghan immigrants who would want to be the very public human face of the country we were about to bomb. I found Professor Daoud Shirzai of Mt. Tabor College, a well-regarded liberal arts school on the edge of the city, because he was the only Afghan immigrant who was putting himself in the public eye. While others whom I called begged me not to publish their names or photos, fearing that their house would be vandalized or their children tormented in school, Professor Shirzai was giving lectures with titles like, "Where is Afghanistan?"

It was easy to access Daoud Shirzai's academic and political persona. He was clearly anti-war, trying to shout out to Americans deafened by their own shock and grief, who believed that the answer lay in bombing Afghanistan. While Bush conjured up images of U.S. bombs "smoking" bin Laden out of his cave, Daoud visualized the more likely scenario of his younger sister and her family in Kabul becoming civilian casualties. That was why he spoke out when other Afghans kept a low profile. Yet Daoud Shirzai's real story was his family: the unmarried man was the patriarch of a patchwork family that included two younger brothers and six nieces and nephews, all of whom he brought out of the devastation of Afghanistan's Soviet War to live in Portland. He had even adopted the nieces and nephews, and raised all of them. He was protective of them, reluctant to talk about them or offer them up to be interviewed. But even as I watched Daoud Shirzai give eloquent, impassioned lectures about the history of Afghanistan, the lack of infrastructure and rampant poverty, about the realities of U.S. foreign policy and terrorism, I couldn't stop thinking about his unconventional family.

As I first began to encounter the Shirzais in that raw time after the September 11 attacks, I felt as if I were slowly being let through a series of doors, past layer after layer of protective walls—and closer to the inner sanctum of the family.

I was also reading everything I could on Afghanistan. Before, I had known what the average moderately informed American knew about the embattled country, which could be summed up in a series of iconic images: *Time* magazine covers from my youth of Soviet tanks rolling across desolate terrain (Afghanistan as a distant bastion of the Cold War). Then, Steve McCurry's ubiquitous green-eyed Afghan girl on *National Geographic* (refugee crisis in an already impoverished region). I didn't hear about Afghanistan much after the Soviets and Americans withdrew, until outcry about the Taliban's rise in the mid-1990s began to build. By then, the reports and secret footage of women in blue burqas being beaten for showing their ankles, or stoned to death for adultery, revealed Afghanistan as a haunted, medieval nightmare that the world forgot. During the long period of American prosperity and the accompanying self-absorption of the Clinton years, we only knew Afghanistan as one of the countries President Clinton bombed right after news of his affair with Monica Lewinsky broke (his "Wag the Dog" moment). In May 2001, the Taliban briefly got the world's attention when they blew up the sixth-century Bamiyan Buddhas as we stood by in horror. I felt particularly sad looking at pictures of the gaping, empty holes in the mountain that once housed the statues, like ransacked coffins. I thought about my devoutly Buddhist great grandmother, and how, if she were alive, she would be heartbroken that something so ancient, hewn from such devotion, was destroyed. What kind of regime would do this to its own country's history?

But like most Americans, my attention once again shifted and by that summer, I was reading far more about Chandra Levy, the murdered intern who had had an affair with a California Congressman, and the O.J. Simpson civil trial. Novelist Rick Moody described the period between the end of the Clinton presidency and September 11 as an "interregnum characterized by a wild desperation," a time of a spiritual thirst. When the terrorist attacks happened, I couldn't help feeling they amounted to a symbolic reckoning for a growing complacency about the world—not the inexplicable act of pure evil unleashed upon the freedom-loving that some characterized it as. This was not something to bring up in polite conversation in the fall of 2001, when patriotic lapel pins, American-flag stickers on cars, and candlelight vigils were almost obligatory, even for those who had previously been skeptical of such displays. So my sadness about the loss of life was compounded by an irrational frustration with the silencing patriotism that gripped the nation. Most of all, I felt my own complicity as an American who had shut off her real awareness of, and connection to, the world to enjoy the ignorant bliss of life here. Why didn't I know more about Afghanistan than just those fleeting images? My own penance, I told myself, would be my upcoming phone interview—my first—with Daoud Shirzai. The title of this talk, "Where is Afghanistan?" taunted me. Did I know where it was—not just geographically, but historically, politically, culturally? I was determined to show him I wasn't another complacent American who had forgotten about Afghanistan—even though I was.

So I read, losing myself in books and articles on Afghanistan. I developed a deep admiration for a nation that had resisted all attempts at conquest, from the British to the Soviets in modern times, as well as Alexander the Great, Genghis Khan and Timur (Tamburlaine) before that. And I was surprised, and unsettled, by the extent of the United States' involvement in the nation's modern conflicts, supplying weapons and training to a *mujahideen* leader named Osama bin Laden to help defeat the Soviets. Afghanistan's "stone-age" poverty did stem in part from its lack of natural resources, as well as its unforgiving climate and terrain. But it was also a priceless piece of land for its geography, as a central location for natural gas export. Similarly, Alexander, Khan and Timur saw its value as a Silk Road trade route—and 19th-century Britain and Russia jockeyed for its potential as a gateway to India in what Rudyard Kipling dubbed the "Great Game."

When the day for my first phone appointment with Daoud Shirzai came, he outlined many of these facts about Afghanistan's geopolitical landscape. I was grateful I could keep up, and eager to show him that I knew what he was talking about.

"Then the country went through the communist coup in 1978, in which the president was assassinated and thousands, if not tens of thousands, of intellectuals and anti-communist activists jailed, taken without a trace or killed," he said.

"And that's when the Soviets came in, followed by the Americans, Charlie Wilson, and the CIA," I chimed in, referring to the Texas congressman who pushed a reluctant Central Intelligence Agency into a monumental covert operation, later immortalized in the book and movie, *Charlie Wilson's War.*

"Right," he said, a touch of warmth burnishing his didactic professor's voice. I savored it.

That was how, from the start, I felt like one of Professor Shirzai's students, eager for his approval. I would learn soon that his nephews and nieces felt the same way. That was just how he was.

And that was how I was let in through the compound's outer door. After a few minutes, he seemed satisfied that I had done my homework, and I mustered the courage to ask about his own family's story.

He hesitated, saying, "Now I don't want to make this too personal or maudlin, but..." He'd talk for a while about the Shirzai family, then try to change the subject back to Afghanistan's history. And I'd ask him again, and he'd reluctantly go back to the story:

The Shirzais's roots were in the Ghazni province, a solidly Pashtun region that reflected the country's largely rural population. Daoud was the firstborn of fourteen, only nine of whom lived to adulthood. They grew up there with no running water or electricity, and Daoud managed to gain an education in Kabul that would lead him to graduate school in Lebanon and the United States. He planned to return to Afghanistan and help his family and country, but his younger brother was killed in the communist coup and several more family members were jailed. He helped two of his younger brothers, Maiwand and Yusuf, avoid being drafted into the Soviet-run army by bringing them to the United States. They watched their country descend into chaos and ruin from afar, helping family members as best they could. In the early 1990s, the brothers decided to bring their slain brother's three children—and three more nieces and nephews, six in total—to Portland to raise and educate. Daoud legally adopted them, aged twelve to seventeen, and all of them went to Mt. Tabor College, where he was on faculty. The youngest would graduate in June.

"But don't make it too focused on me," he said again.

"I think it's important to tell your family's story, to help people understand," I said.

"Why?" he said. "I want them to understand that bombing a country that has already been bombed to the ground will do nothing to curb terrorism."

I felt like I had been called on in class. My mouth was dry. I cleared my throat.

"Because the people you want to reach, not the ones who will choose to go to your lectures, but the ones who will happen upon the story in the paper as they eat their toast and drink their coffee in the morning, are used to being complacent about Afghanistan," I said. Before September 11, that was me. "They won't care unless there is a human face on the story," I added, cringing a bit at using my editor's terminology. "Your family's story represents what Afghanistan has gone through."

"OK," he said. I felt victorious. He sighed loudly. The line went silent for a while.

"My adopted country is waging war on my country of origin," he said. "It's a very difficult position to be in."

He had been matter-of-fact, scholarly even, when talking about his brother's death, about the sacrifices he made raising six adopted children—including not having a wife or family of his own. But now, hearing his sharp voice dampened by exhaustion, I no longer felt like a student, or a reporter. The grief, and the conflicting feelings, of the past two weeks welled up, and I saw a place to channel them that—unlike aggressive patriotism, anthrax scares and invading Daoud's country of origin—made sense to me. I wanted to bear some of his hurt, as penitence for being a complacent American. For allowing Afghanistan to come to this, for being part of the media machinery that hadn't cared until we needed to put a human face on the country we were about to bomb.

I wanted my editors and readers to feel something, to hurt in the way he did, just a bit.

I had made it past the outer wall. Next, I asked to accompany him to one of the daily lectures he was giving on Afghanistan, usually at anti-war-oriented gatherings at churches and local universities. He had a meeting at Portland State University, which was right next to my office, before the lecture at a left-leaning church across town. He said he'd give me a ride there from the university. Stephanie, the photographer, agreed to meet me at the church to shoot the speech.

When I arrived, five minutes late, he was standing in front of the building he'd ask me to meet him at, looking at his watch. He was a smaller man than I had imagined from the resonant voice on the phone. The authority he projected and my sheepishness about being late—few people in Portland were that punctual—caused me to hesitate. "Daoud Shirzai," he said in greeting, extending his hand and motioning with his head as if to say, *Let's go*, at the same time. In time, I'd get used to his brusqueness. We walked together to the parking garage. He was professorial and rumpled at the same time, in a navy blue blazer, light blue shirt, patterned burgundy tie and khaki pants. They were neither outdated nor fashionable, and later, his nieces and nephews would joke to me that "Uncle Daoud has only one outfit." I pictured the *Inspector Gadget* cartoons of my youth, in which the cyborg Sherlock Holmes-esque hero would open his closet with rows of identical tan trenchcoats and say, comically, "I wonder what I should wear today?"

Daoud walked quickly, his build compact and square-bodied, but not fat. He had told me he was fifty-eight over the phone. (Later, one of those same nieces would say, "Uncle Daoud has been fifty-eight for three years now!" In truth, few of the Shirzais were born in hospitals and rural

Afghans rarely tracked birthdates, so there was room for poetic license.) His sweep of side-parted hair bore not a hint of gray, and his brown face was tired, but relatively unlined. He had a strong, furrowed brow and eyes so dark they looked black.

"So," he said as we approached the parking garage, "what's your assignment for tomorrow's *Oregonian*? Will it be good enough to reprint in *The New York Times*?"

He read the *Times* daily, and for him, it was the best of American print journalism—though he complained that all newspapers were biased, and none of them had adequate international coverage.

"Well," I said, "I don't have anything in tomorrow's paper because I've been dispatched to focus solely on, um, you."

He raised his eyebrows.

"Not just you, of course, but this story that gives people a window into Afghanistan through your family." He hadn't given me the OK to meet his brothers, nieces and nephews yet, and I hoped to slip in the idea.

He inhaled sharply, and opened his mouth to speak, in protest perhaps, but then was stopped in his tracks as he surveyed the row of cars in front of him. His hand flew up to the side of his face, index finger extended.

He forgot where he parked his car. Lucky break.

"I hate it when that happens," I said playfully.

He didn't look at me, made a "huh" noise to himself, and started walking tentatively in one direction. As we rounded the corner, he relaxed and started walking faster, stopping at a bright red Volvo sedan. Turbo. He didn't seem like a red-car kind of guy.

"Ooh, don't get into a car with Uncle Daoud. He's a scary driver." That was another one of the "Uncle Daoud jokes" the nieces and nephews would tell me later, which weren't really jokes at all, but ways in which they affectionately made fun of him. "His mind is always on a million other things, and he drives *fast*."

I, of course, didn't realize this until we were in the car, whipping out of the garage exit and onto Southwest Broadway, tires squealing.

"You seem to be doing a lot of speaking these days," I said, gripping the inside door handle.

"At a time like this, I want to be in Afghanistan, not here. I cannot be there, so I do what I can. I accept every invitation to lecture because it is what I can do," he said, the rhythmic nature of his speech syncing with his sudden, signal-less lane changes as he darted through rush-hour traffic.

"How long have you had this car?" I said. "It…handles well."

He shrugged his shoulders. "One of my nephews chose it for me a couple years ago," he said, accelerating through a yellow light turning red. "I know nothing about cars."

When we arrived at the church, it was packed. The audience was just about entirely white, which wasn't a surprise for an anti-war-themed event at a Methodist Church in Portland. The minister, a tall, enthusiastic man in a polo shirt and jeans, gave Daoud a bear hug when he walked in. Daoud accepted the warmth of the greeting, pumping the reverend's hand a couple times in a handshake as he pulled away. As I followed him into the makeshift green room, he pulled out a yellow note pad and started to flip through pages and pages of longhand notes written in precise printed script, tilted at a slight forward angle like warriors marching into battle. "Do you still work at the homeless shelter here?" I asked. I had done some research and found an article from a few years ago about how he took a part-time job as the church shelter's morning janitor and sent the money home to his family in Afghanistan. The story had painted a picture of a solitary man sweeping and scrubbing in the dawn hours with the nobility of a Benedictine monk.

He raised his head and turned to me, surprised. "Oh. You read that. I had stopped over the summer because I was traveling, and meant to come back in the fall. But then—well, I've had other things on my mind of late."

He went back to studying his notes. I thought about the article. Something about his monastic humility—cleaning toilets, scouring shower stalls, telling the homeless children to stay in school—felt like more than just charity. It felt like self-imposed penance. But for what?

As he approached the lectern to speak, I found a place on a folding chair in the audience of a couple hundred. On the side of the room, I saw Stephanie poised with a camera and waved at her. I wanted to tell her about the white-knuckled drive to the church, and how Daoud had worked as a janitor here, but there would be time for that later.

As he started to speak, it became clear that the notes he had reviewed were unnecessary. He never looked down. He began with a history of Afghanistan, just like he started our phone conversation, but drew the audience in with details like, "My sister, who is illiterate because she never had the educational opportunities that girls here take for granted, lives near the Kabul Airport, which has been identified as a target for bombing. It is people like her who will suffer if we invade, not Osama bin Laden and al-Qaeda." Audience members nodded vigorously. He had the booming, deliberate voice of a skilled public speaker. His hands gestured emphatically as he scanned the crowd, letting his dark-eyed gaze settle upon certain individuals now and then. They sat up straighter, like *they* were about to be called on.

As the forty-five-minute speech wound into its second half, the tone changed. He had transitioned into a far-reaching, heady geopolitical survey of the highly disproportionate distribution of wealth in the world, and the United States' complicity in brutal conflicts from Central America, to Iran and Iraq, to Israel and Palestine (he said "Palestine" with a stress on the last syllable, as if to say "*not* 'Palestinian territories'"). Here, some of the audience members started to squirm. It was not even two weeks after September 11—even liberals had teared up when Congress sang "God Bless America" on the steps of the Capitol. They came with their sympathy for Afghanistan and their generalized opposition to war. But they weren't ready, with their raw wounds, to hear someone criticize the United States without qualifiers. Doing so felt akin to saying that the terrorists' actions were justified.

"Right or wrong, terrorism is a statement of the desperate," he concluded. "I don't know how you stop terrorism, but if we continue to contribute to the world's inequities, we are part of the problem." A small number of people jumped up and applauded heartily. A much larger number clapped politely but looked uncertain. A handful sat with their arms across their chests, eyes boiling and mouths agape. A few walked out before he started taking questions.

For the most part, those who stood up during Q & A represented two opposite extremes—neither of which were really asking questions: Some were like the middle-aged woman in flowing natural fibers who gushed, "We are praying for your family, and especially for all those poor Afghan women and girls who may only know the devastation of bombs before they feel the sunlight on their unveiled faces." And others were like the college-aged, sandy-haired man, who stood bolt upright, jaw clenched, as he introduced himself with a Jewish surname and said, "How dare you continue to spread your anti-Semitic views on Israel at a time like this, to even so much as imply that U.S. policy to Israel brought on these senseless, evil acts."

Daoud had little patience for either of them. He nodded and "mm-hmm"-ed as the first woman gushed and replied with a simple, "Thank you. Next question?" To the angry man, he didn't yield, unleashing a stream of facts and statistics about the numbers of displaced and killed Palestinians, citing bin Laden's 1998 manifesto that specifically listed the U.S. support of Israel as one of the grievances that merited retaliation. "It's not justification for terrorism, but it's naïve to think that Israel is not a reason that terrorists attack the United States," he said, staring straight back at the questioner.

This same speech would later draw death threats, and as he spoke more, the warnings began arriving at some high-profile venues before he did. One night, he would be accompanied by a plainclothes policeman to a speech in central Oregon. Daoud didn't seem to mind the danger, nor the demanding speaking schedule on top of his full-time teaching. The lecture treadmill distracted him from the grief he felt as he anticipated the inevitable: Bombs falling once again on his homeland.

When I found him after the speech, his face slack with exhaustion, I introduced him to Stephanie. "Did you get my good side?" he said. She flashed her winning smile, made all the more endearing by her wispy, pixie-like haircut. I, on the other hand, always struggled with my long mane of thick hair that tried to go in too many directions at once, like my own frenetic nature. She had a naturally demure way about her, something I lacked completely. I felt a pang of envy. Why hadn't I been privy to this charming, joking Daoud?

He turned to me: "What next?"

Your family, I thought, but bit my tongue, remembering his reaction in the parking garage. "What do you suggest?" I said.

"OK, here, write this down," he said, and started reciting a phone number from memory. I scrambled to find a blank page in my notebook.

"My brother Yusuf. He'd like to speak to you."

I suppressed a smile. Yusuf was the youngest of the three brothers here in Portland. I wondered why he had not offered up the middle brother, Maiwand. But I didn't want to push my luck, so I didn't say anything. The door to the next wall was opening.

I met Yusuf in the musty Portland State building where he was preparing pictures for the next "Where is Afghanistan?" event, a photo exhibit combined with a lecture by Daoud. He was threading string through frames for hanging, wearing a faded yellow T-shirt and olive-green canvas pants. For all that Daoud was compact and professorial, Yusuf was gangly, with an artist's unfettered energy. He was thirty-nine, tan-skinned with deep-set dark eyes, a long face and a trimmed full black beard. Handsome in an odd, awkward kind of way. He was a computer engineer by day, but the ease with which he handled the frames made clear he had hung more than a few exhibits before.

We had barely gotten past our initial greetings when the photos grabbed my attention. I unstacked them, careful not to leave fingerprints on the glass. They were portraits taken in Afghanistan and Pakistan. They had a candid feel to them, even when the subjects were looking directly at the camera. They were old men, young men, children, a few women—some, not all, in the midst of modestly pulling a scarf over their faces. There was something similar about all of the people, something in their dark eyes and strong noses. "Who are they?" I asked.

"They're all family, some in the village, some in Kabul and others who settled in Pakistan during the wars," he said. "But I'm not telling people that. I want them to think of these pictures as if they could be anyone from Afghanistan."

No one, except for a few of the children, smiled for the camera. It was easy to project onto the serious faces and assume they were sad. But, like in my own Chinese culture, Afghan people did not traditionally smile for pictures. And having a photograph publicly displayed, especially for women, was a far more significant and intrusive thing than for

Americans. That was part of Yusuf's motivation for not identifying them as family.

Our conversation followed the photographs, as he talked his way through them. He told of his own childhood and adolescence amid bombings, gunshots and rockets of the Soviet War. He had lost friends and acquaintances to violence and landmines. Everyone had. You just got used to the sound of gunfire, he told me. "You didn't think about the possibility of dying because then you'd just stop living," he said. "I'm tired of watching Americans get so beside themselves over a few thousand deaths on September 11, when that kind of random killing has been happening every day in Afghanistan for nearly a quarter century."

I raised my eyebrows and scribbled in my notebook, expecting him to say, "Don't quote me on that." He didn't. (I ended up not using it, for his own sake, though I secretly admired his honesty.)

Growing up in the village, Yusuf idolized Daoud, his eldest brother who was twenty-plus years his senior, more a local legend than a real person to him. Daoud was studying abroad by the time Yusuf was born. He sent Yusuf Lee jeans, Tinker Toys, and Silly Putty. Then the family moved to Kabul, into a house Daoud bought for them. "Then my brother was lost. Daoud told you about that, right?" He stopped threading the strings through the frame, a shadow crossing his eyes.

I wanted to say no, so I could hear Yusuf tell me, but it was a rhetorical question. Of course Daoud had told me. But "was lost" caught my ear as an unusual phrase—shouldn't he have said, "Then we lost my brother"?

"That," he said, "really tore the family apart. But there was no time to grieve or heal, because the Soviet war started and we were just trying to stay alive."

The draft started, and communist officers would visit homes, looking for boys old enough to fight. At seventeen, Yusuf would surely be recruited, but he bought himself extra time by getting a fake ID and shaving extra close. Finally, the family decided it was time for him to get out of the country. Maiwand, after having been jailed once for writing anti-communist graffiti in a school bathroom a few years earlier, had already left and joined Daoud in Oregon. Yusuf would do the same, but he'd have to sneak out, hitching rides and climbing mountains on foot to get to Pakistan. He fled with just a knapsack full of Afghan bread, large oblong pieces of thick flatbread that could be rationed by tearing off one small chunk at a time, and his most prized possession—a collection of Afghan and Indian pop music tapes. "I still have those tapes," he said.

He pulled a picture from the pile, a portrait of a long-nosed, flint-eyed man with a long white beard and face furrowed beyond age. The man wore an elaborately wrapped gray turban. He squinted into the camera as if he weren't sure what to do in front the lens. It occurred to me that Yusuf's portraits looked candid because many of his subjects had rarely posed for photos. The man's head and shoulders occupied the left foreground. A rippling wheatfield and azure sky extended over his right shoulder. "That's my father. He died in 1995," he said. I looked at his father's face and the landscape, and could almost feel the dry, hot wind that swept over the wheat and caught the length of stiff fabric trailing from his turban. What had this man seen in his life? Could he imagine the life and world his sons inhabit now—both their American lives, and this unsteady, uncertain time, on the edge of another war?

Yusuf pulled out another framed photo, this one in black and white, of a group of turbaned, bearded men sitting on the floor of a mud-brick building. They wore traditional tunics and loose pants with wool shawl-like blankets wrapped around them, their knees tucked up at various angles. The half-dozen men looked uncertainly in various directions, as if they weren't sure if the picture was being taken. Except for one man—the only one with just a mustache, not a beard—who stared directly at the lens, challenging the photographer. His square jaw was set, his arms crossed over his knees.

"He's the first man I've seen in these pictures without a beard," I said. "And why is he angry?"

Yusuf laughed. "That's because he's my brother, Maiwand. I mean, he's not wearing a beard because he's Maiwand—he was visiting from the U.S. And he's not angry, that's just how he always looks."

"Oh," I said. The elusive Maiwand. "Is that why I haven't met him yet?"

Another laugh. "Well, sort of. He's really emotional right now. All of this—the way people are reacting to September 11, to the idea of invading Afghanistan—really hits him hard. He's angry at a lot of people and things right now. Not the least of which is the American media."

"Oh," I said again. "Does he want to talk to me?"

"I think he will. Daoud's talking to him about it."

As I waited for Maiwand, something remarkable happened. I started getting calls and e-mails from the nephews and nieces.

"Hi, my name is Mohib Shirzai. You can call me Mo. My Uncle Daoud told me to call you."

"Hi, I'm Laila. My uncle is Professor Daoud Shirzai. He gave me your number."

Receiving these calls, I felt like yet another curtain was parting, and he was now entrusting me with his adopted children. But what about Maiwand? I thought about his stare in that photo, the steely face that peered out from under the turban.

I had peeled back the next curtain, to find another wall, higher and more daunting yet.

At the end of September, U.S. planes and troops built up in the region and refugees poured out of Afghanistan. I felt the futility of Daoud's speeches, and of the article I had published, using his and Yusuf's interviews, to preview the "Where is Afghanistan?" exhibit and lecture. Maiwand's silence continued.

I had imagined Daoud waiting for the inevitable airstrikes as I wrote, "For Afghans, family is everything. And to be far away when family members are in danger is to be an empty shell without a life force—without a heart."

"That was a pretty good story. Accurate," Daoud called me to say. "The line about Afghans and families was true. Almost good enough for *The New York Times*."

Normally, this would have irritated me—I, too, admired *The New York Times'* reporters, but was not trying to imitate them. Yet I was eager for his approval and charmed by his idiosyncrasies. I told him I'd like to delve deeper into his family's story, to write more as the inevitable war started.

"OK," he said. "Write this number down."

I copied the number, holding my breath.

"Maiwand," he said. "I think he's finally upset enough about the plans to bomb to talk to you."

I exhaled. I had passed another test. I wasn't sure if Daoud was joking, but I triple-checked the number, drawing and retracing a thick rectangular frame around the digits on my notepad as I said goodbye. I took a couple more deep breaths, rehearsed what I would say, and called. Voicemail. I left the most rational-yet-compassionate, non-rambling message I could, given that I was sweating in my air-conditioned office as I delivered it.

Midday on October 7, television networks announced the start of airstrikes. "AMERICA STRIKES BACK," one cable station's banner read. It slammed onto the screen with dramatic music every time there was an update on the bombings. On October 8, Maiwand called.

"Hi. So you want to talk to me," he said, his voice raw.

We agreed to meet the next day, at a Starbucks on the ground floor of a glass-encased office tower, across from the building where he worked as a city engineer. We met each other in the line, standing next to a newspaper display with an aerial infrared photo of flattened jets at Kabul Airport. All of planes belonged to the national commercial airline, Ariana Airlines. Maiwand held the paper—the newspaper I worked for—up an inch and shook his head. "That's disgusting," he said, dropping it back on the stand as if it were toxic. I didn't ask if he meant the bombing, the newspaper, or both, because I was afraid to hear the answer. "They're *commercial* airplanes," he muttered as he turned to the barista to order. "Venti coffee, please. Extra hot. With room."

Though I had just met Maiwand, his intimate knowledge of Starbucks lingo seemed to him what a red, turbo-charged car was to Daoud. He looked more like his older brother than Yusuf did, with a similar compact build, but more athletic. He was forty, and had married an Afghan woman from Pakistan a few years ago and just become a father to a baby girl four months ago. Without the turban and the mustache from the picture—he was now clean-shaven—he looked completely different, younger, though his expression still held traces of that scowl. He had a thick mop of wavy black hair that had been tamed into a professional-enough hairstyle, accentuated by the Portland business-casual uniform: light blue button-up shirt, khakis, brown Timberlands that looked office-acceptable but could go for a hike. I wanted to feel comfortable with him. But the raw edge of his anger rested between his thick brows, knitted in concentration as he drank his giant cup of coffee. A piano player in the building lobby was offering up gentle classical music against the trickle of fountains. It didn't feel like the United States had just started a war. We settled on some couches overlooking the lobby.

Maiwand vented for a while about *The Oregonian*: jingoistic headlines and photo choices, the pro-war stance of certain columnists. Didn't they understand that Saudi-born terrorist in hiding—not Afghanistan—had attacked the World Trade Center and Pentagon? I nodded, took it all in, and didn't protest.

"I'll be honest," he said. "I've never liked your paper."

"That's fair. They do sign my paycheck," I said. "But if I told you I was confident that I'd have almost total autonomy to report and write this story about your family the way I wanted to, right down to the headlines and the photos, could you take a chance and trust me?" My editor and Stephanie were on my side, so I wasn't overstating my creative control.

"And what way is that?"

"I just want to tell the story of what happened to your family in Afghanistan through the wars, and how that shaped your patchwork family here," I said. "I think anyone reading that would come away with a better understanding of the place and people we're bombing now."

"OK," he said, more quickly than I expected—the same way Daoud did. "What do you want to know?"

Maiwand described his youth in the village and then Kabul, a bridge between Daoud and Yusuf's versions. He was attending the Kabul Polytechnic University when the communist coup started. "And then my brother was lost," he said. "And everything changed."

"He was lost," I tested out this odd phrasing in my own mouth.

"That's what we say," Maiwand said. "His body was never found. He was taken, put in prison, and two years later they handed his wife his clothes, his wedding ring, and watch and told her to stop looking for him."

In Afghan culture, he explained, when a death is unconfirmed, everyone says that person is "lost" until both parents die. "My mother is still alive. She still says her son disappeared."

"Daoud doesn't say that," I said. Could I push him a bit on this? Somehow, the khakis, Timberlands, and Starbucks cup made me feel like I could.

"No. But that's Daoud," he said. "You can bet he says 'lost' in front of our dear mother."

We talked about the nephews and nieces. He said raising them was a sacrifice. "I would have never married so late," he said, the anger dissipating from his brow, replaced by something new. Was it regret? Melancholy? Tenderness? "I would have never waited so late to start a family."

Soon, I was asking to see his daughter's picture, and all traces of the scowling, turban-wearing man disappeared. The first real smile broke out across his face. It was a toothy, almost giddy, smile. My own anxiety unfurled. He pulled out a day planner he had been carrying, and in a pocket on the inside flap of the front cover, there were two photos of a plump-faced baby girl in the hospital, with a mass of black hair much like his own, only baby-fine. Unlike most squinty-eyed newborn pictures, in this one her eyes were wide open, chocolate brown, and full of wonder.

"She's beautiful," I said, really meaning it.

Her name was Aisha Diwa. Her middle name meant *light*. "She changed everything," he said. "Not just for me. I mean, I became a different person, a softer person. But I think she's good for the whole family."

The family in Portland had become a somewhat unnatural, if tight-knit, product of untimely death and war, he said. It had been a long time since new life was breathed into it. Everyone badly needed pure joy, and that's what Aisha brought. They needed her now more than ever.

"She's the only one who doesn't know this bombing is going on, the only one who has a chance to grow up knowing only a peaceful Afghanistan," he said. "And we, we needed to see that this is how life happens, how family happens. She's much bigger now. You should see her."

"I would love to, and to meet your wife," I said.

"We get the whole family together for dinner on Sundays. This Sunday should be interesting," he said, explaining that they needed to make a call to Pakistan to check on news about relatives in Kabul near some of the bombing sites. Phone lines and Internet had been cut off after the invasion started. "You're welcome to join us. If you're free."

If I'm free? I had learned all I could in a matter of weeks about Afghanistan, about the three Shirzai brothers, and their stories. I was the guest whom they had let in past the courtyard wall, invited into the home—and finally, allowed to peer through the curtain between public and private, what Tamim Ansary described as "the hidden world inside our compounds." Now, as war began in their homeland, the Shirzais were letting me in. Maybe they trusted me, maybe they needed a witness to their pain and worry, maybe they just needed to share something with someone other than lectures and exhibits about their country and war. I was not stepping into their hidden world to learn more about Afghanistan, or even to share in their news from Pakistan and Kabul. I needed to see, as Maiwand put it, "how family happens." And in this raw time at the cusp of war, the bonds that held them together within the walls of their home were all that was certain, unchanging.

Lisa Vaas

The Saddest Tootsie Pop Ever

I was a little sad that my therapist wasn't moved by a photo of my lollipop, the saddest Tootsie Pop ever. She wanted instead to talk about my dad, and how scary it was that he yelled at me for no good reason when I was a little kid, and how scared that must have made me feel and how I must have blamed myself, how I must have internalized that and how that dynamic must still be playing out in my skull now, but it was hard to focus on what she was talking about. My skull and I were floating on a hypoglycemic fuzz cloud, overcome by affection for my snacks.

I had wafted into therapy after having sat at a table in the coffee shop for what felt like a very long time. As I sat in the coffee shop, picking shreds of glued-on wrapper off this particular Tootsie Pop, it struck me that it was the saddest member of its clan. I realized that I had been picking at its wrapper for quite awhile, ignoring the fresh, crispy cellophane-clad organic lollipops arrayed on the coffee shop table beyond, any of which would have been easy to get out of its wrapper, any of which were eager to help out by increasing my blood sugar and thus feeding my glucose-starved brain.

The brain doesn't work well without glucose. The central nervous system—the brain and spinal cord—is unique in being the only organ that lacks the capability to store glucose. Whatever your brain needs, food-wise, jet fuel-wise, make-me-think-thoughts-and-process-language-wise, it better be there ready to soak up from your blood, or you're going to be as stupid as a rock. You're going to get to the counter at a deli and some guy in a white cardboard hat is going to ask you what you want and you're just going to laugh at his hat and fall in love with him, overwhelmed with compassion for those who are forced to wear white cardboard hats, and then you'll stare at all the beautiful containers of greasy orange and white and brown lumps and globules and fall in love with the luscious glowing blobs as if somebody had finally adjusted the light dimmer in the gallery's back room and now the photorealistic painting of a crumpled brown paper bag was leaping out at you with shadow and crease and depth and breadth and soul, soul, soul. Somewhere inside those clear containers of food is the key to unleashing you from this rapture, but the ability to discern where has evaporated, and, truth be told, do you really want to go?

Yes, you do. You're going to want, desperately, to say to the white paper hat person something more intelligible than just me-give-some-thing-ummm. That, that, that, oh, yes, but, there's that, and you'll laugh at your own garbled head, your own garbled situation, and once in a thousand times maybe the guy you're talking to will figure out you're diabetic, but then he'll get all his own brain's messages scrambled, and so he'll try to give you Diet Coke, thinking, Well, she's diabetic, so she can't have sugar, right?

You'll shake your fuzzy head, because even a stupid rock like you knows that won't help. There's something in your DNA that knows that fake sugar isn't real sugar. But who can blame the white paper hat people? It's not their fault. It's all confusing. People keep trying to be helpful, to share cures, such as the guy who wanted to date me and who was very proud of developing a diabetic diet of raw vegetables churned up in a blender. It cures diabetics, he said. One tries to be polite. One says, Yes, that's marvelous, you can indeed cure that kind of diabetes with a sewage spill of raw vegetables, that Type 2 kind of diabetes, but no, not this kind of diabetes, this Type 1 kind being more of a professional-level diabetes. The kind where your pancreas has gone on strike, isn't making any insulin, refuses to be coaxed into making insulin by a vat of raw vegetables. Less of a dilettante's diabetes. One hates to be snobbish, but, well, there you have it. It's not the couch-potato kind of diabetes, it's the other kind.

But, still, you are in the deli, with the Diet Coke paper hat guy. You've got potato salad and egg salad and juice and chocolate bars staring at you and can't seem to begin the conversation with the snacks to tell them which snack in your private beauty snack pageant might be chosen to save your life.

You say, "Ummm." Blink. Blink. Blink.

About 15-18% of any glucose that goes into your belly—French baguettes and potato chips and carrots and Whoppers and popcorn and pizza and Tootsie Pops, those wonderful little corn syrup orbs that can bounce around at the bottom of your backpack for months and still be ready to help out, if perhaps a bit melted, if perhaps a bit adhered to by detritus, by unnamable grit, by molecules shed by books and crumbs left by other members of the snack clan, successive generations of which have always squatted in your equipage, cheerful gypsy snack travelers come to spend part of their life cycle in your belly, bless them, bless them and their progeny, bless their shameful high-fructose illicitness, bless their photosynthesis-derived glucose molecules, those sixlet chains of carbons holding hands with doubled-up dozens of hydrogens and then streams of septuplet pure oxygen, bless the glucose, bless the sugar that the people whose hobby it is to suggest laws want to rip out of cafeterias and government snack machines, to tax because they think it's evil and will make us fat, bless the rich gulps of dark sinful carbonation erupting from a Coke, fizzling your nose and tasting of caramel and sputtering like a small volcano of life, bless the fuel it feeds the brain, bless it, bless it all—about 15-18% of that ingested glucose goes straight to nourish the brain during the absorptive period of digestion. The brain doesn't store glucose, it burns it, burns it on the high holy altar of cognition, burns it as it flips Cartesian cartwheels and writes or reads sentences like these.

The brain is, therefore, extremely sensitive to reduced blood glucose levels. This impairment of cognition presents an interesting conundrum, given that cognition enables self-diagnosis and treatment. You don't have much else to tell you when your blood sugar is low besides your brain, or a gadget to test your blood sugar, but again, what tells you to use a gadget to test your blood sugar? A sugar-plumped, glucose-stoked brain.

I was fond of this particular Tootsie Pop. It struck me as being ludicrous like a scrotum is ludicrous, an aged senility implicit in wrinkled folds of melted, veiny purple that rose in small dusk-purple mountain ranges, scraps of paper like swaths of fog adhering where no paper should be. A crumb of cognition made me self-aware at some point, made me question my fixation on unpeeling the atmospheric haze of wrapper, made me look up to the table's surface, spread with a horizon of lollipops that were waiting to serve. But because hypoglycemia is what it is—the flip side of attention deficit, more an attention surplus disorder, as it were—I then fell in love with my brain's obviously debilitated state, and with the pathetic state of a long-forgotten piece of candy, as if they were related by blood: one an enfeebled, starving brain and the other this wrinkled, sticky, forgotten piece of candy.

That's how I chose not to treat the hypoglycemia, but to instead photograph the Tootsie Pop.

The last person I loved, as love-filled people do, consoled me when he broke up with me. He told me that I was beautiful and smart.

"So what?" I said. "That doesn't make me happy."

"What's so great about being smart?" I said. "Stupid people are probably much happier than smart people. Smart people think about things too much."

I ate the Tootsie Pop. I packed my things up, left the coffee shop and walked down the block to my therapist's office. As I walked, the loving warmth of stupidity lingered, and I picked the paper out of my back teeth.

It made me wonder about the neuroanatomy of hypoglycemia. It made me wonder over the parallels between meditation and hypoglycemic-induced stupidity. Aren't they similar? The stilling of the mind's chatter, either by meditative focus or sugar deprivation? It made me think of the work of Dr. Norman Doidge, or of Dr. Jeffrey M. Schwartz, neuroanatomists who write about the power of the mind to alter the brain's mappings, to still the hyperstimulated alarm systems of the brain—the amygdala and the caudates—and about the ability of obsessive compulsive disorder sufferers to soothe and shrink their own swollen caudates through guided meditation. Could a similar rewiring be evident in a brain exposed to a forced state of meditative awareness and focus, such as hypoglycemia? Does a lifetime of diabetes and exposure to hypoglycemia make somebody more prone to using alternative synapses? To quieting the ringing alarms of the brain's alarm systems?

What I wanted to communicate to my therapist, to Susan, had something to do with the rapture of stupidity.

Although some relatives of diabetics disagree with their findings, scientists have failed to discern permanent brain damage from recurrent episodes of low blood sugar in the brains of diabetics.

I didn't peel off all the flaking skin of that thing. I put the entire thing in my mouth. I take entire things and pull them into me. I draw in the grit and the purple mountain majesties and the wrongness and the storm and the blood-sanctioned sugar, the photosynthesized godhead, and I absorb it all, nutrition and offal, without label or thought.

I feed myself.

Irène Mathieu

The Most Beautiful Woman I've Ever Seen

You were the most beautiful woman I've ever seen. You reminded me of me. Half your face from behind the denim jacket of some bald-headed Anglophone, eyes curving into the half-moons that mine make when I laugh, hair streaming, streaming like a piece of the universe. Like instead of being born miniature, wrinkly, wet like the rest of us, your mother made you with her hands, picking for your hair the raw darkness of midnight just above the ocean. You couldn't tell by looking that your laugh was forced. You could tell by feeling, though. You'd practiced, I know, in front of a cracked mirror, some of your sister's lipstick like a red tattoo as you flirted with the spotted glass. Your practice showed. The way you let your lips curl so wide that I could see a flash of gums, that's what made it look real; that's how I laugh. I used to hate when people caught that moment of abandon on camera instead of a measured smile of pure whiteness, but now I know that I am the most lovely when I let my measurements go.

I kept sneaking glances at you and him. He looked like a little boy who has won the school lottery. His turn with the goddess. His night to feel large. The opposite of love isn't hate. It's power.

When he excused himself to the restroom I watched you, alone. You were the most beautiful woman I've ever seen. You reminded me of me the way you looked, staring suddenly sober at the street. You reminded me of me when I am with only myself, and the conversation we are having could change the course of things. I wanted to outbid him. Offer you a thousand pesos to go with me into the night, to make our own sweet place where we could let the little girls inside own everything we saw. We could have owned the restaurant, the one across the street, all the park benches, and the guitar-strumming trio paying homage to Santo Domingo's obsession with Iberia. We could have owned ourselves, which we owe ourselves, could have lain in each other's arms like sisters from before birth.

When he returned, you remembered. There again the half-moons waning, there the hands on his shoulders to make him feel large. There again the steady cession of the opposite of love, from your goddess fingertips to the center of his pride. We always remember how to eat. I wished instead that we were in my kitchen. That, laughing, we were becoming family as we shared secret tricks—how my mother taught me to press garlic open with the flat belly of a knife; how yours taught you to put the *plátanos* in oil for just enough time until hot-hot, we scooped them, jumping, out. I wished I could take you to the roof of my apartment, could put my arm around your shoulders and keep you from being cold, ever. I wanted just to look at you, the most beautiful woman I've ever seen. You reminded me of me, the way your hair offered no explanation and even less apology. The way your nose was a question mark. The way your lips were a birth canal for voice, for language, for love. I wanted just to sit, silent, with you. I wanted you to keep me from being scared, ever.

History was haphazard in its becoming. The most beautiful woman I've ever seen, and you were bending love aside in order to eat. Me, who reminded me of you, with a whole menu at the start of each day. With more than enough pesos to outbid the little boy with the bald head. With more than enough.

When you got up to leave with him, I wanted to yell. If our eyes met once, it would be over: the waiting hotel room, the sweaty sheets, the cession of the opposite of love, flowing steady like a leaky faucet until there was nothing left, the sunset ember of a cigarette after, the predictable snores like the putt-puttering of an old car, the tears stained Maybelline black, the flipping the pillow over, the not sleeping, the sweaty sheets wrapped around your beautiful legs, the half-moons turning up to the sky behind the window glass, the not sleeping, the feet like restless ghosts wanting back what your hands ceded, the inexplicably waking up, the putt-puttering over, the suit back on, the sheets dry, the pesos in your hand, the free breakfast, the coffee included, and the back home, peeling off jeans like paint and sleeping, sleeping. If our eyes met, it wouldn't happen. You would still have had it all and we would have found the long-lost sister from before birth, from the place where we are a nestled piece of the universe, waiting to be shaped by our mothers' hands.

When you got up to leave with him, my heart broke. The shattering cracked my breath; bits of metal lodged in my lungs and oxygen was suddenly lead. I was amazed you didn't hear the sound, didn't turn around. If our eyes had met, we could have been different. My heart broke when I saw your back, unapologetic hair and painted pants. You were the most beautiful woman I've ever seen. I loved you at first sight, and our eyes never met. When you left with him, something of me left, too. You reminded me of me, before birth. Before we had names, fingernails, tears, blood, collarbone hollows, spinal cords, or question marks. Before we were born, we were already beautiful.

Contributors

Contributors

Paul David Adkins graduated from Washington University with an MFAW in poetry in 1991. He has poems published or pending in *Artful Dodge*, *Rattle*, *Crab Creek Review* and *Chattahoochee Review*. He received a Pushcart Prize nomination in 2004.

Kelli Allen is an award-winning poet and scholar. She is the Managing Editor of *Natural Bridge*, a journal of contemporary literature.

Greg Billingham is a recent graduate of the University of New Hampshire with a BA in English. He is currently living, working, and writing in New Hampshire. Previous or forthcoming publishing credits include *Poetry Quarterly*, *Existere*, *Chaffin Journal*, *White Whale Review*, *Grasslimb*, and *The Sierra Nevada Review*.

Angie Chuang lives in Washington, D.C., and is on the faculty of the American University School of Communication. She was a newspaper journalist for thirteen years and is now working on a book-length work centered on a 2004 trip to Afghanistan and the family she stayed and traveled with there. Excerpts have been published in the anthologies *Best Women's Travel Writing 2011* and *Tales from Nowhere*.

Jenna Devine is a junior English major at Princeton University, where she was awarded the Ward Mathis Prize for Best Undergraduate Short Story in 2009. Jenna has studied creative writing with Jeffrey Eugenides and Joyce Carol Oates. This is her first non-Princeton publication.

Ruth Foley lives in Massachusetts, where she teaches English for Wheaton College. Her recent work is appearing or forthcoming in *River Styx*, *Measure*, *The Ghazal Page*, and *Umbrella*, which just nominated one of her poems for a Pushcart Prize. Ruth also serves as Associate Poetry Editor for *Cider Press Review*.

Timothy Kercher is in the process of moving to Kyiv, Ukraine, from the Republic of Georgia, where he has been editing and translating an anthology of contemporary Georgian poetry. He completed his MFA at Vermont College of Fine Arts in January 2010. His poems and translations have appeared in or are forthcoming in publications such as the *Atlanta Review, Poetry International Journal, Nashville Review, The Evansville Review, Ellipsis: Art and Literature, Los Angeles Review, Sierra Nevada Review,* and *Eclectica.*

Christopher Linforth is an MFA fellow at Virginia Tech. He is the editor of the forthcoming book *The Anthem Guide to Short Fiction* (Anthem Press, 2011). Christopher's work has been published in literary journals including *Denver Quarterly, Permafrost,* and *Camas.*

Irène Mathieu is a writer from Virginia and a 2009 graduate of the College of William & Mary (BA in International Relations). Her essay was written during a year in the Dominican Republic, where she completed Fulbright research on gender and tuberculosis. Previous publications include poetry in the magazines *34th Parallel, Magnapoets,* and *Damselfly Press,* and photography in *34th Parallel* and *The Meadowland Review.* Irène was a finalist in the Jane's Stories Press Foundation's 2010 poetry contest.

Jenn Monroe is an assistant professor of writing and literature at Chester College of New England. Her work has recently been published in *Danse Macabre, Sakura Review,* and *The Chamber Four Literary Magazine,* and earned second place in the Borges Poetry & Prose Contest sponsored by *Caper Literary Journal.*

Kristine Ong Muslim authored the full-length poetry collection *A Roomful of Machines* (Searle Publishing) and the e-chapbooks *Our Mr. Flip* (Scars Publications), *Graphic* (Sikworms Ink), and *Smaller than Most* (Philistine Press). Her prose and poems have appeared in publications such as *Boston Review, Contrary Magazine, Hobart, Moon Milk Review, Narrative Magazine, The Pedestal Magazine,* and *Southword.* She has been nominated five times for the Pushcart Prize and four times for the Science Fiction Poetry Association's Rhysling Award.

Erin Elizabeth Smith is the author of the book *The Fear of Being Found* (Three Candles Press 2008) and the chapbook *The Chainsaw Bears* (Dancing Girl Press 2010). Her poetry has appeared in journals such as *32 Poems, The Yalobusha Review, New Delta Review, Water-Stone Review, Third Coast, Crab Orchard,* and *Willow Springs.* Erin holds a PhD in

Creative Writing from the University of Southern Mississippi and is a lecturer in the English Department at the University of Tennessee.

Ryan Stone is the author of the short story collection *Best Road Yet* (Press 53, 2010). His fiction has appeared in publications including *The South Carolina Review, The Madison Review, Natural Bridge,* and many others. He teaches writing and literature for Danville Area Community College.

William Stratton currently lives and writes in Newmarket, NH, where he is pursuing an MFA at UNH. His poems have previously been published and are forthcoming in *The Cortland Review.*

Jamie Thomas studied at Western Michigan University and University of Houston. He lives in Detroit (for now) and is a visiting professor in the Languages and Literature Department at Ferris State University. A Recipient of an Academy of American Poets Prize, his poems have appeared in such journals as *32 Poems, 5 AM, The Missouri Review, Rattle,* and *Verse* and online at *Verse Daily.*

Christopher Tozier happily lives deep in the sand pine scrub between Paisley and Cassia, Florida. He has been selected as a 2011 State of Florida Artist Fellowship recipient. His poems have appeared in journals such as *Tampa Review, Post Road, Saw Palm, San Pedro River Review, The Literary Review, Cream City Review, The Florida Review, Maryland Poetry Review,* and *The Wisconsin Review.* He graduated from the University of Wisconsin-Madison Creative Writing and English program.

Lisa Vaas is a freelance writer and an MFA student working on a collection of creative nonfiction pieces at Goddard. She has been published in *Fence,* the *Best of Fence Anthology, Binx Street,* and *Pitkin Review,* where she also recently served as a fiction editor.

Ronald Wallace co-directs the creative writing program at the University of Wisconsin-Madison and edits the University of Wisconsin Press Poetry Series (Brittingham and Pollak Prizes). His 12 books of poetry, fiction, and criticism include *Long for This World: New & Selected Poems,* and *For a Limited Time Only: Poems,* both from the University of Pittsburgh Press. Ron divides his time between Madison and a 40-acre farm in Bear Valley, Wisconsin.

The Lindenwood Review

The Literary Journal of Lindenwood University
Fiction • Poetry • Essays

Submit

The Lindenwood Review is an annual print journal and welcomes submissions from both new and established writers. We look for fiction with believable characters and a vivid story; poetry with original, interesting use of language; well-crafted, honest essays; and mostly, work that moves us.

Submissions should be emailed to TheLindenwoodReview@lindenwood.edu. Visit http://TheLindenwoodReview.blogspot.com for full submission guidelines. Contributors receive two copies of the issue in which their work appears.

Submission period: July 15 through December 15
We will respond to all submissions by March 31.

Subscribe

Issue 1 of the *The Lindenwood Review* — $7.00
Purchase Issue 1 and Pre-Order Issue 2
(to be published spring 2012) — $12.00

Please include your mailing address with your order. Checks should be made payable to Lindenwood University and mailed to:

The Lindenwood Review
Beth Mead, Editor
400 N. Kingshighway
St. Charles, MO 63301

The Lindenwood Review is published by the MFA in Writing program at Lindenwood University. Our program focuses on the practice and study of creative writing. We offer personalized instruction in small workshop sessions featuring a wide range of genres—fiction, poetry, creative nonfiction, scriptwriting, and journalism—with the option to emphasize in a chosen genre. Online classes are also available. Visit us at http://LUmfa.webs.com.

Beth Mead, Director
bmead@lindenwood.edu
LUmfa.webs.com

LINDENWOOD
St. Charles, MO
www.lindenwood.edu

Lindenwood College Library, c.1910. (Image: Mary Ambler Archives, Lindenwood University)

Subscribe to *The Confluence* and Hold a Library in Your Hands

Want to know how our region became the way it is? Subscribe to *The Confluence*.

The Confluence is a new semiannual publication from Lindenwood University. It's lively and engaging and deals with the history and science of our region. Our Spring/Summer 2011 issue commemorates the 150th anniversary of the Civil War with articles about the war in St. Louis and St. Charles.

Every issue of *The Confluence* is profusely illustrated, and reflects some of the best and freshest scholarship on our region, presented in compelling and interesting ways.

Readers of *The Lindenwood Review* can now subscribe to *The Confluence* for just $15—that is 25 percent off the regular subscription price.

Please subscribe online through www.lindenwood.edu/confluence. When finishing your purchase, enter code "LURev01" to receive your discount. You can start receiving your next installment of the history, art, architecture, and business in our region with our current edition.

the *Confluence*
Where Ideas
Converge

LINDENWOOD

Eve Jones | Bird in the Machine

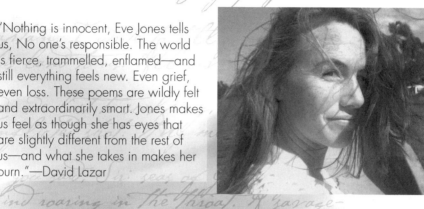

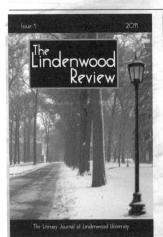